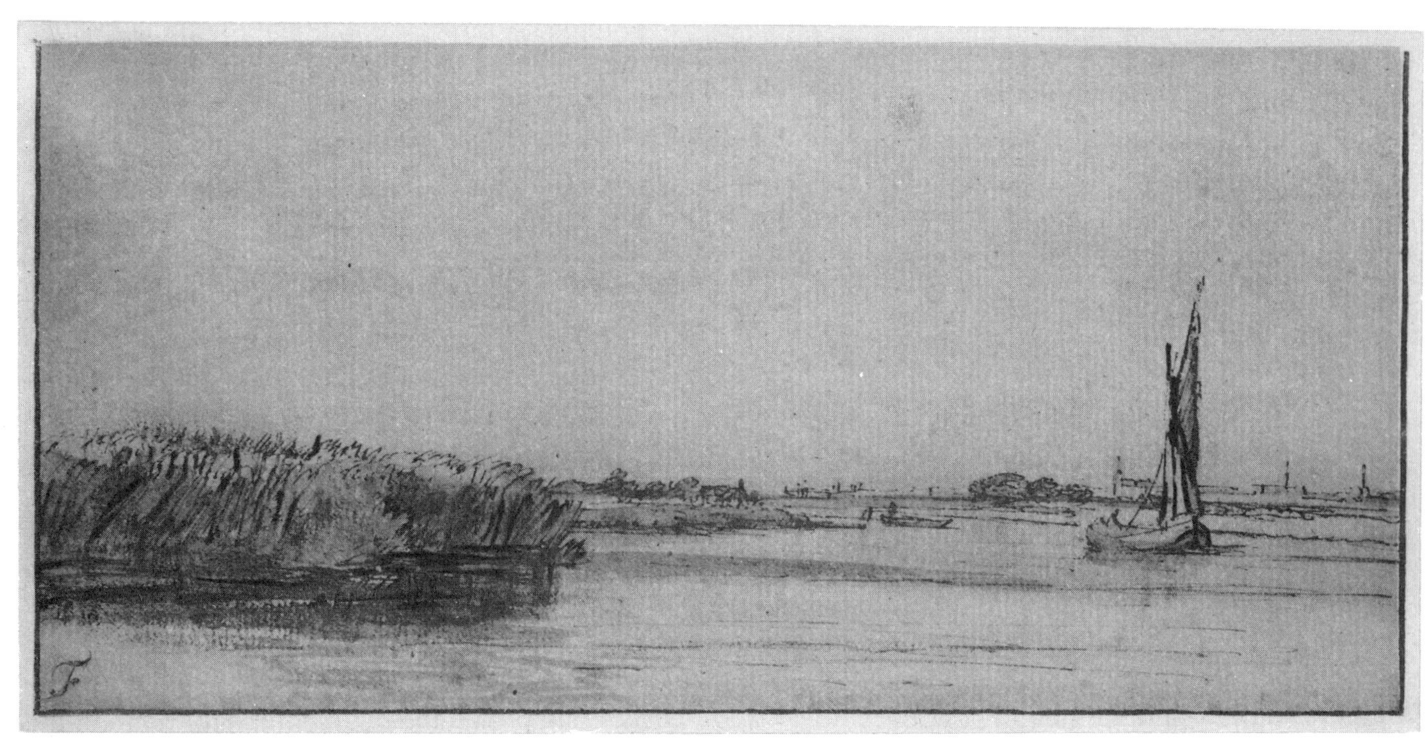

View of a Lake with a Sailboat on the Right and High Reeds on the Left. Ca. 1650. Pen and wash in bistre. 88 x 181 mm. Chatsworth Settlement.

REMBRANDT
LANDSCAPE DRAWINGS

60 Works by
Rembrandt van Rijn

Dover Publications, Inc., New York

Publisher's Note

Rembrandt van Rijn (1606–1669) is one of the supreme landscape artists of all time because of his great empathy with natural settings and deep understanding of the place of man's works among those of nature. The Dutch countryside was a source of constant inspiration to the artist all his life, and he would return repeatedly to the same site, experimenting with new ways to capture the quiet grandeur of the scene before him. The works included in this volume (which, as is generally the case with Rembrandt drawings, can only seldom be identified as direct preliminary sketches for larger works, but were obviously done chiefly for their own sake) are arranged in chronological order. They range in date from the more naturalistic sketches of the mid-1630s to the vibrant, masterful compositions of the late years, in which the world is seen bathed in an almost magical light.

No drawing is included here that is not considered perfectly genuine by the major Rembrandt scholars. In the captions, the original dimensions of the drawings are given in millimeters, height before width.

Published in Canada by General Publishing Company, Ltd., 30 Lesmill Road, Don Mills, Toronto, Ontario.

Rembrandt Landscape Drawings, first published by Dover Publications, Inc., in 1981, is a new selection of drawings. The identifications of the subjects, and the captions, are based on those in the two-volume work *Drawings by Rembrandt*, by Seymour Slive, published by Dover Publications, Inc., in 1965. The Publisher's Note has been prepared specially for the present edition.

International Standard Book Number: 0-486-24160-2
Library of Congress Catalog Card Number: 81-66493

Manufactured in the United States of America
Dover Publications, Inc.
180 Varick Street
New York, N.Y. 10014

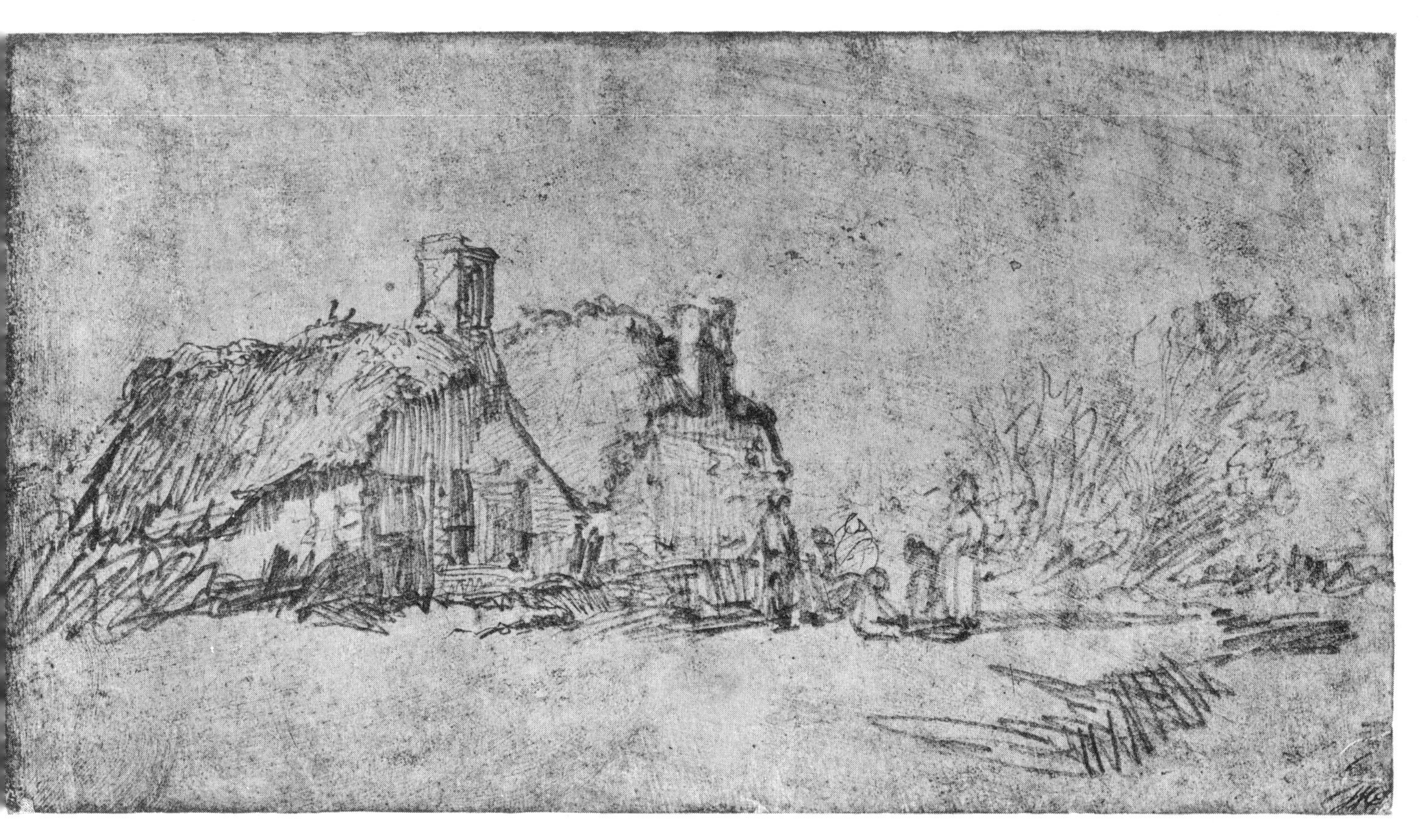

1. LANDSCAPE WITH TWO COTTAGES. Ca. 1635. Silverpoint on white prepared vellum. 109 x 192 mm. Kupferstichkabinett, Berlin.

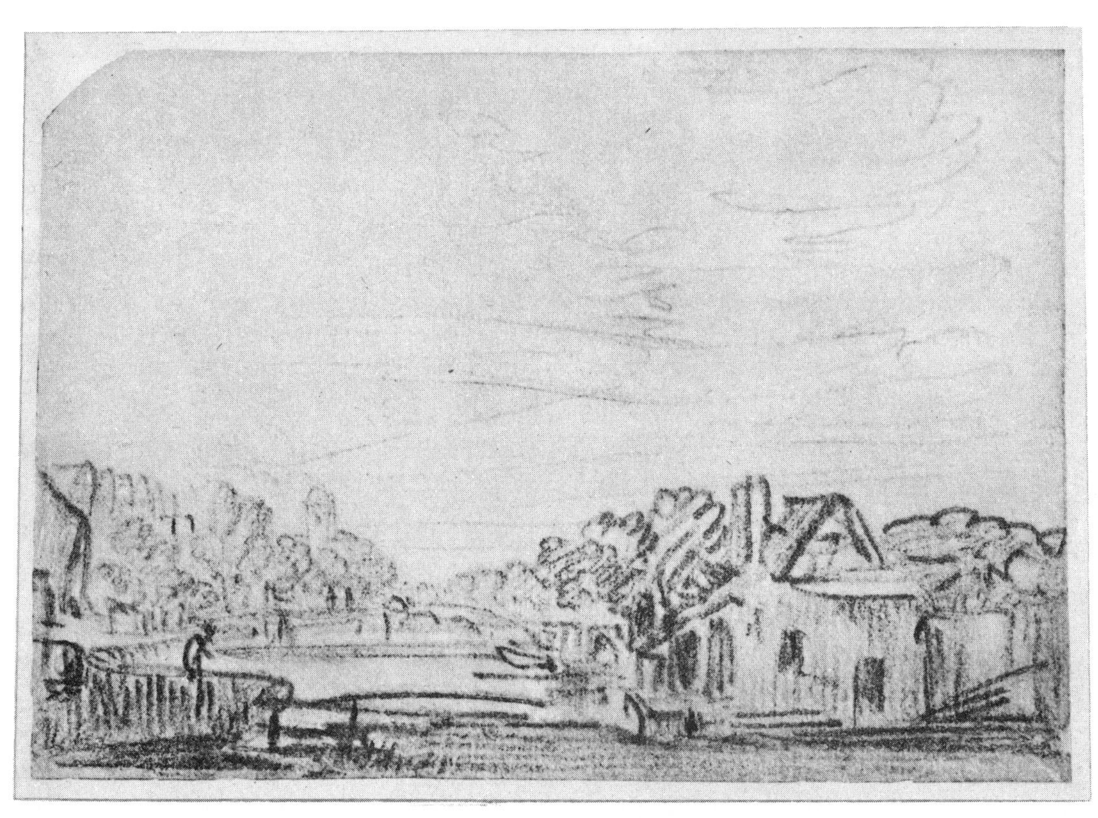

2. A Canal with a Bridge in the Distance. Ca. 1640. Black chalk. 98 x 138 mm. Kupferstichkabinett, Berlin.

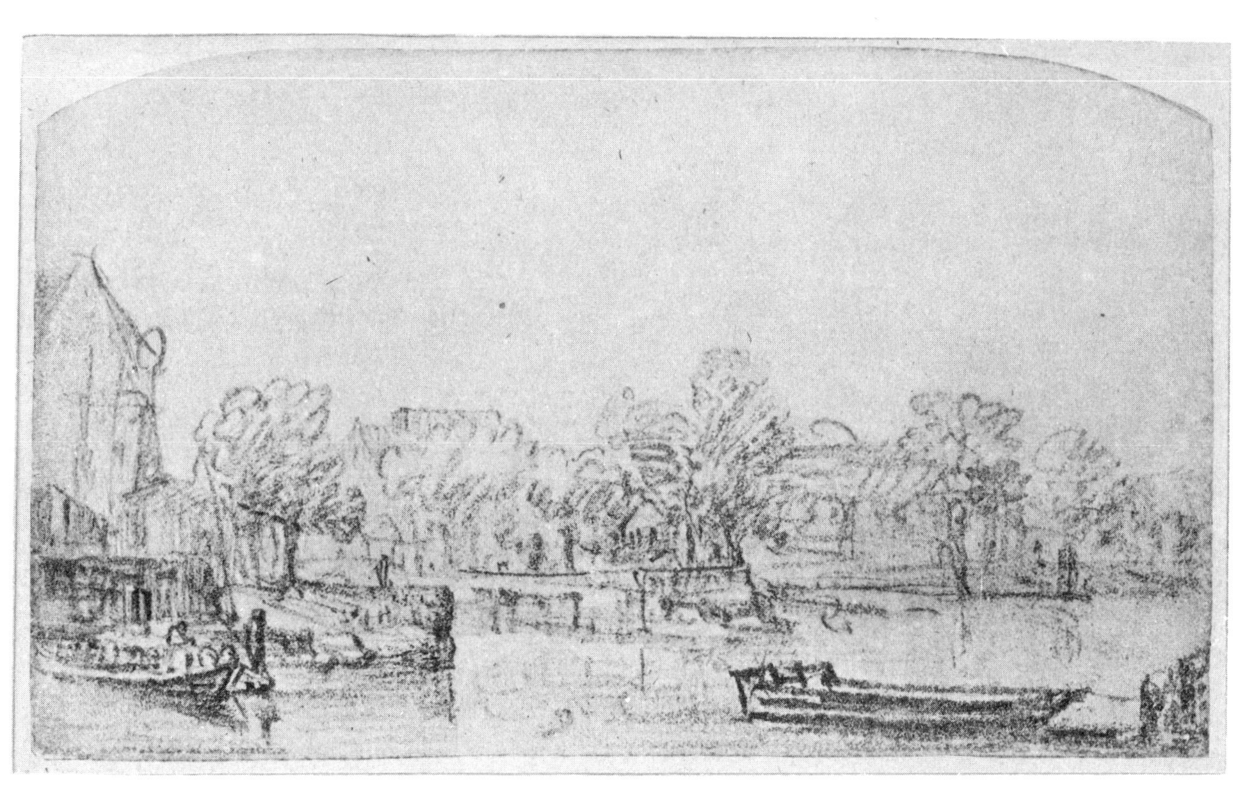

3. View of a Canal with a Boat in the Right Foreground. Ca. 1640. Black chalk. 94 x 156 mm. Kupferstichkabinett, Berlin.

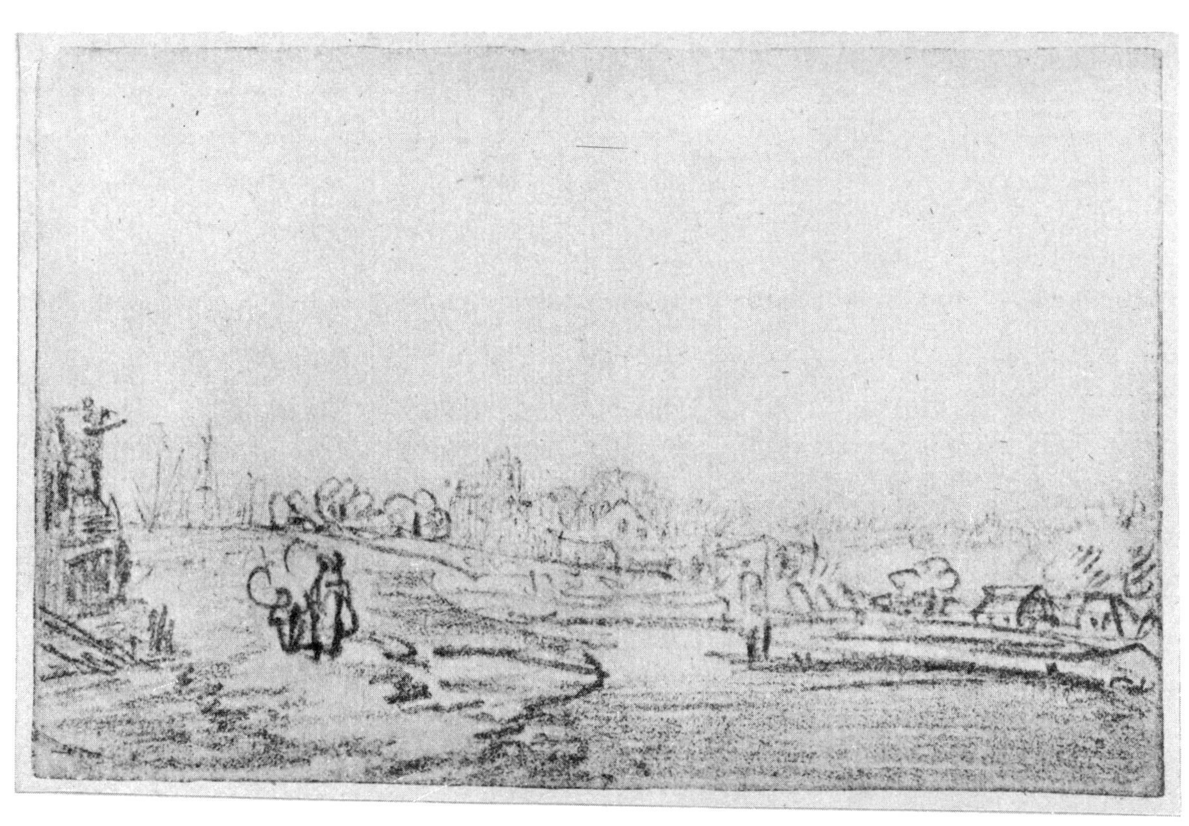

4. Landscape with a Canal Leading Toward a Town in the Distance. Ca. 1640. Black chalk. 100 x 150 mm. Kupferstichkabinett, Berlin.

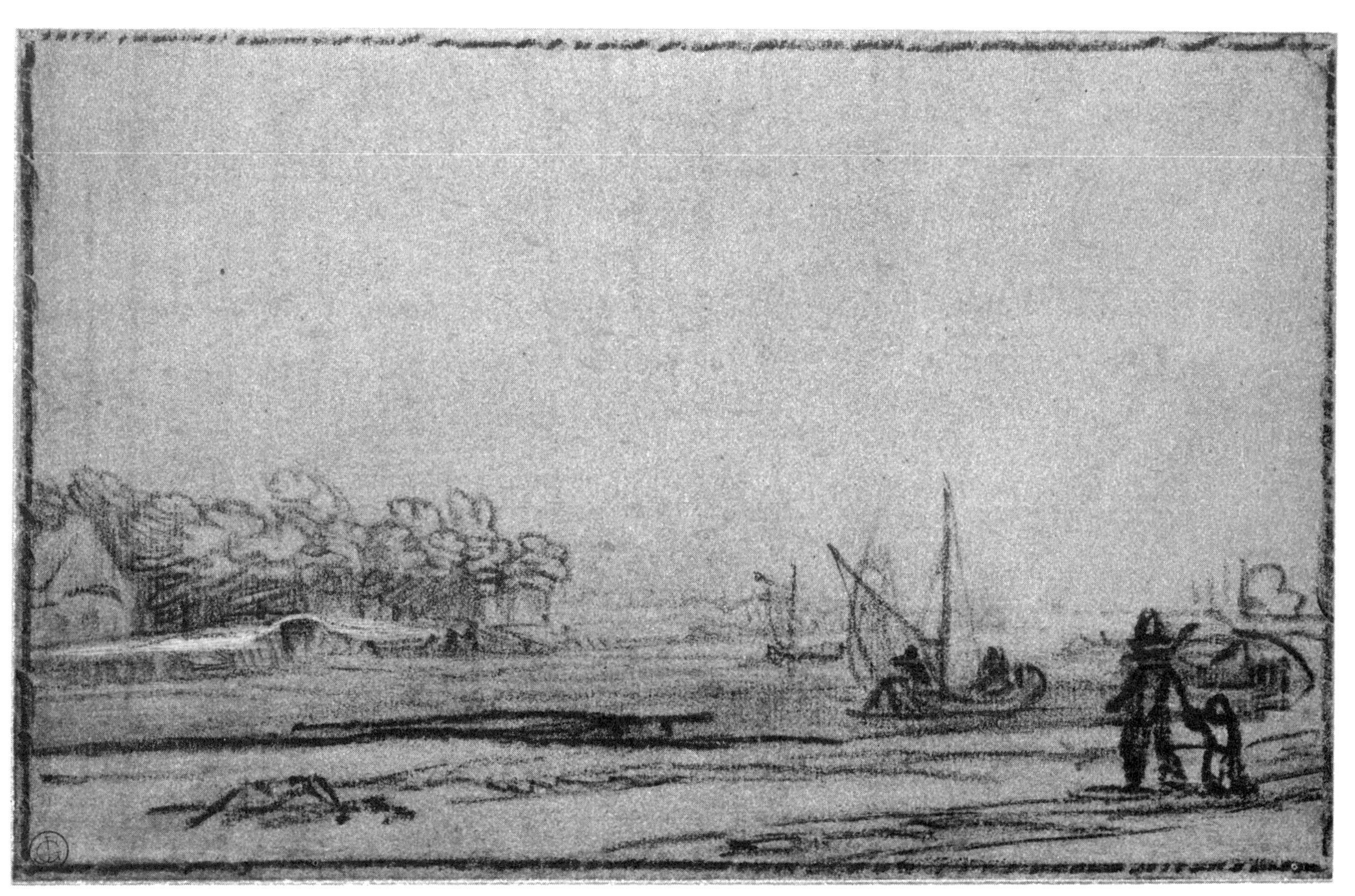

5. A VIEW OF THE AMSTEL. Ca. 1640–45. Black chalk with touches of white on the left. 119 x 185 mm. Kupferstichkabinett, Berlin.

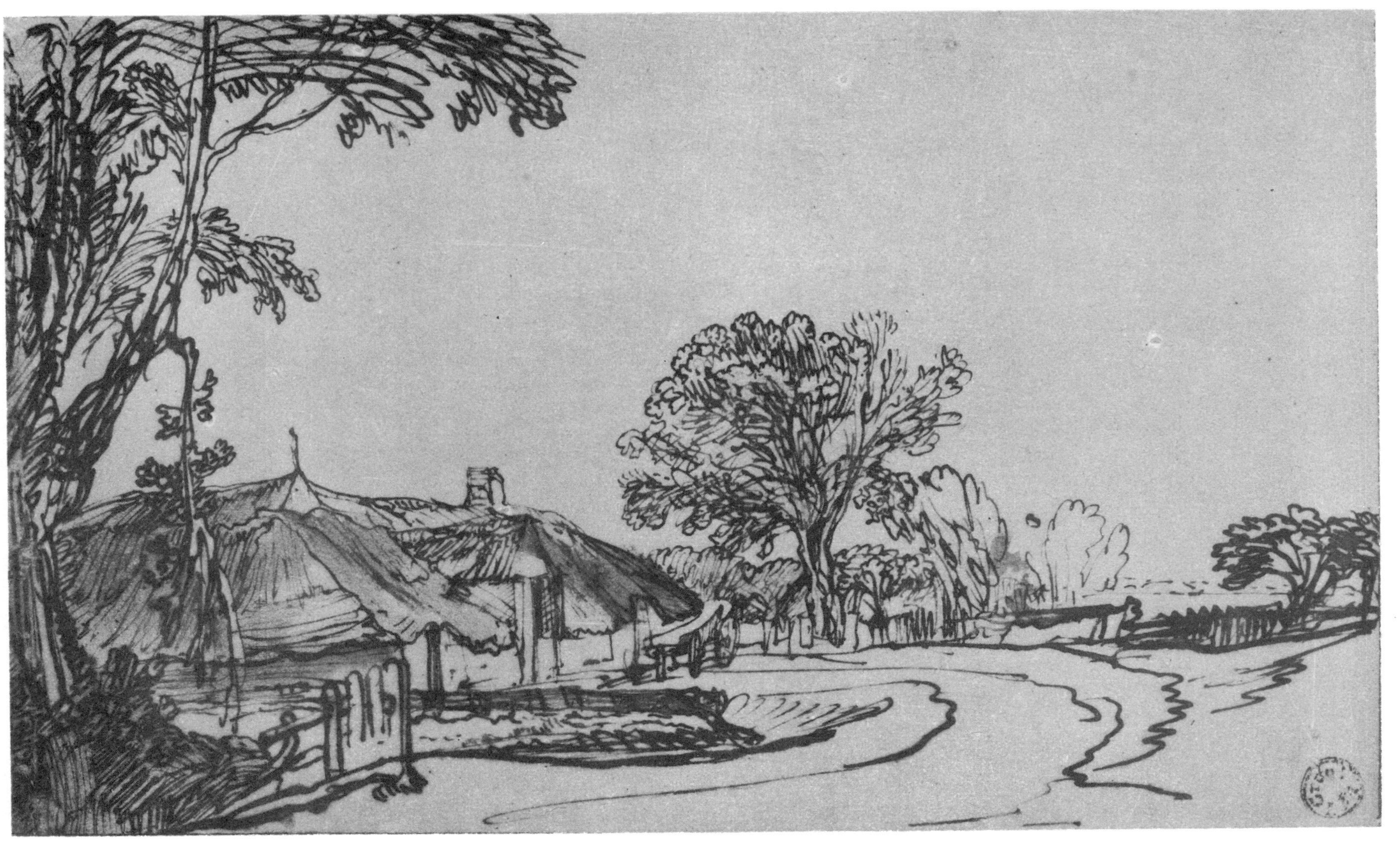

6. Cottages Beside a Road. Ca. 1640. Pen and wash in bistre. 141 x 237 mm. Louvre, Paris.

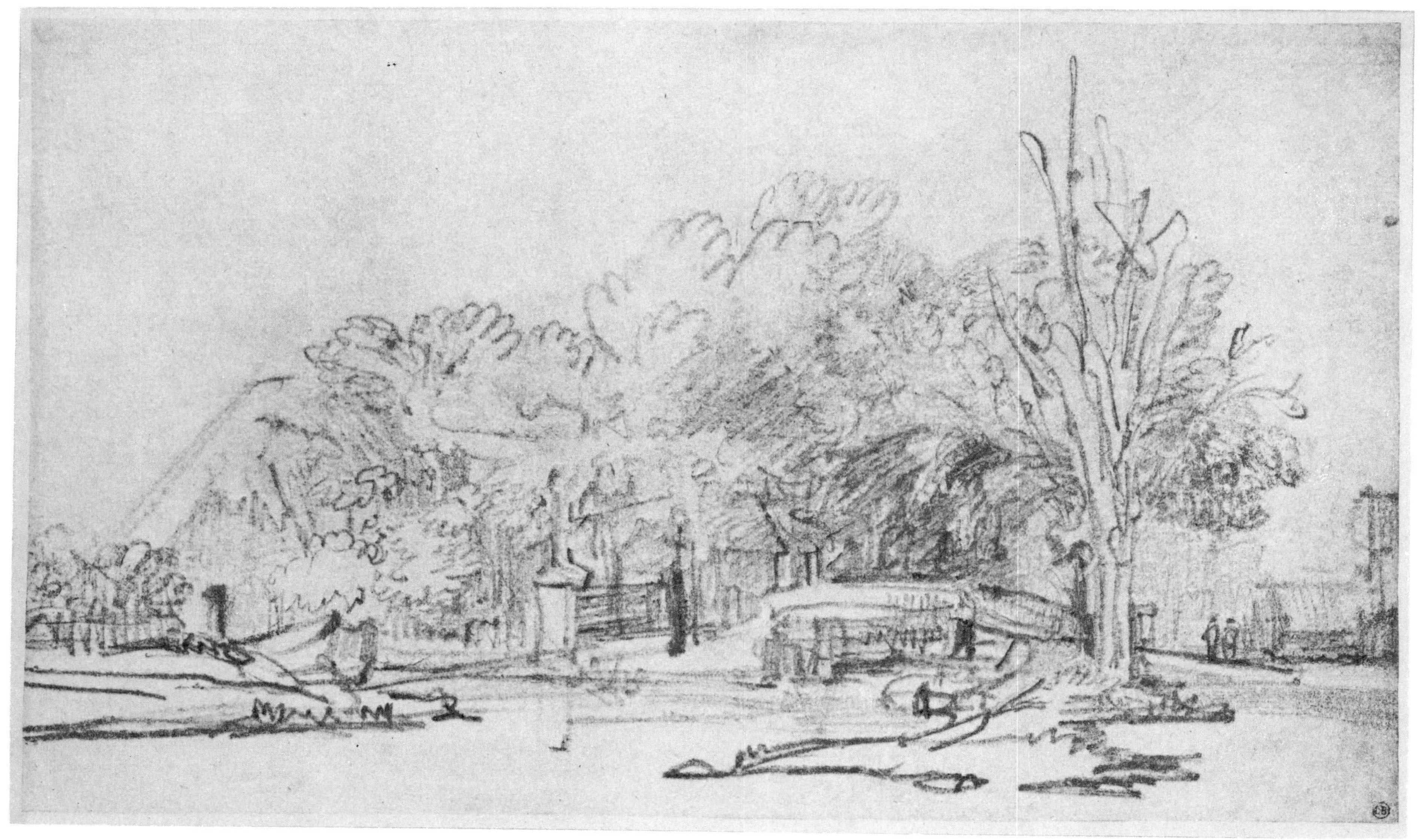

7. House Amidst Trees. Ca. 1642–45. Black chalk. 175 x 297 mm. Musée, Bayonne.

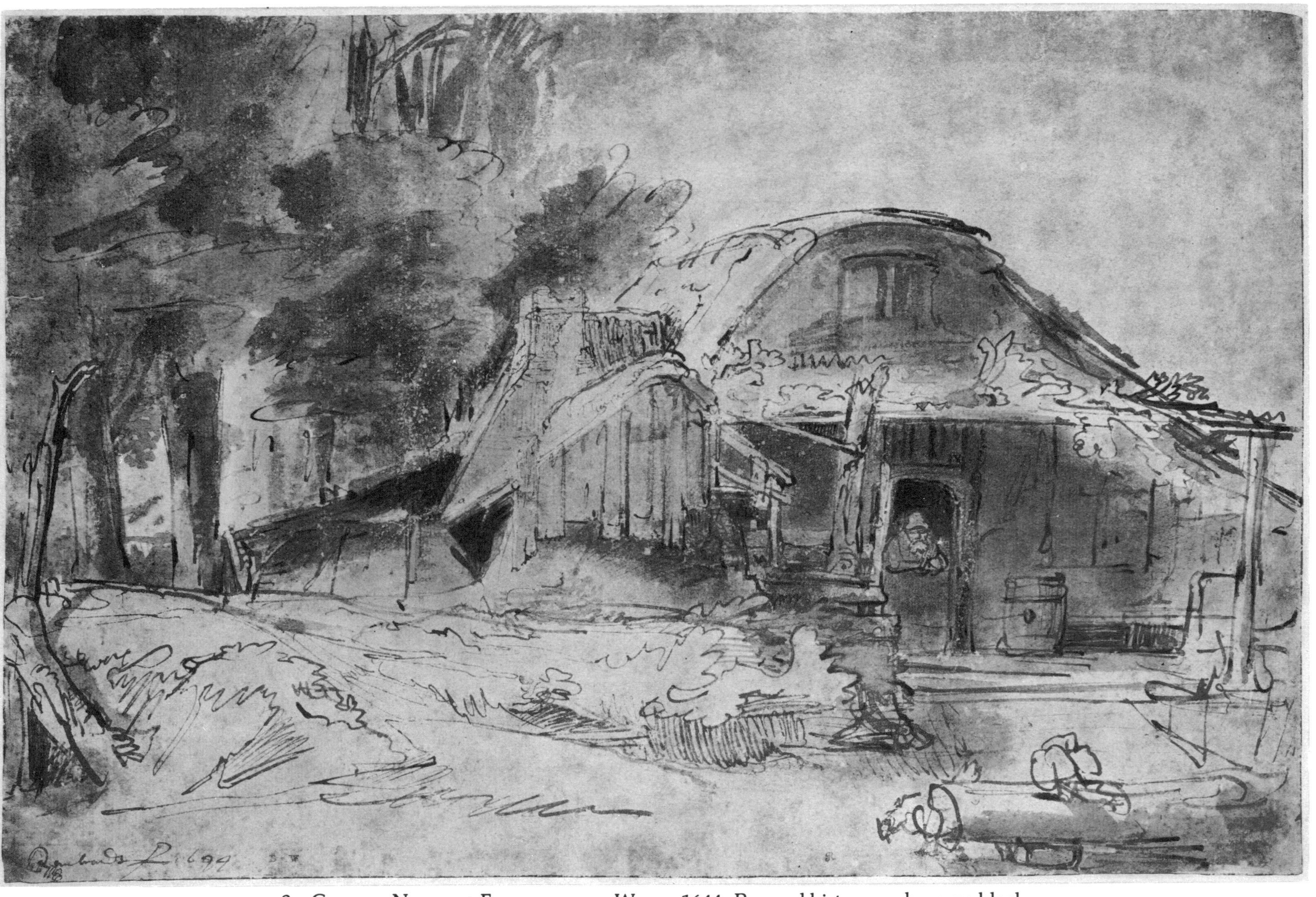

8. Cottage Near the Entrance to a Wood. 1644. Pen and bistre, wash, some black and red chalk. 298 x 452 mm. Robert Lehman Collection, New York.

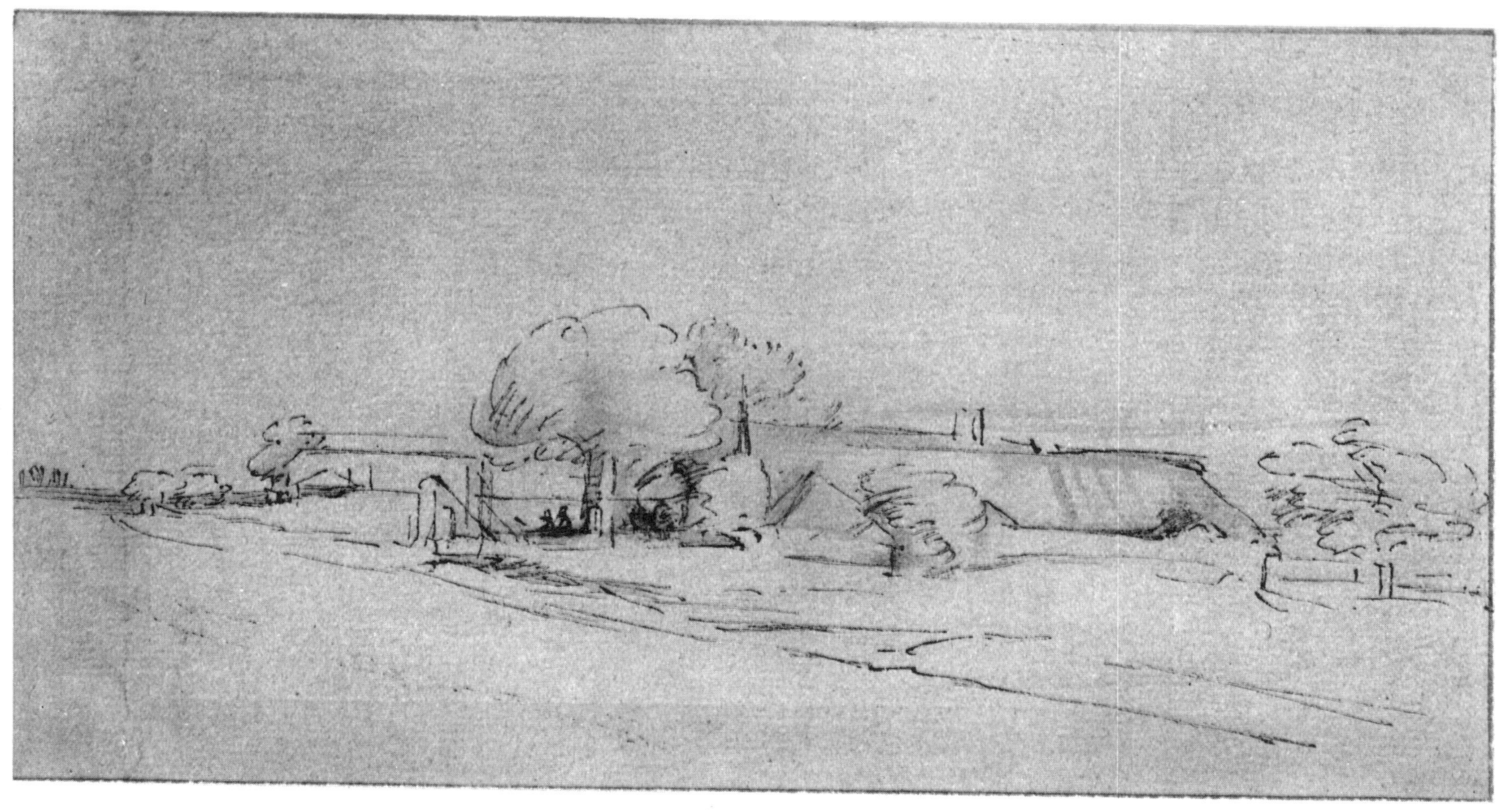

9. Farm Buildings Near a Canal. Ca. 1647–50. Pen and wash in bistre. 117 x 222 mm. British Museum, London.

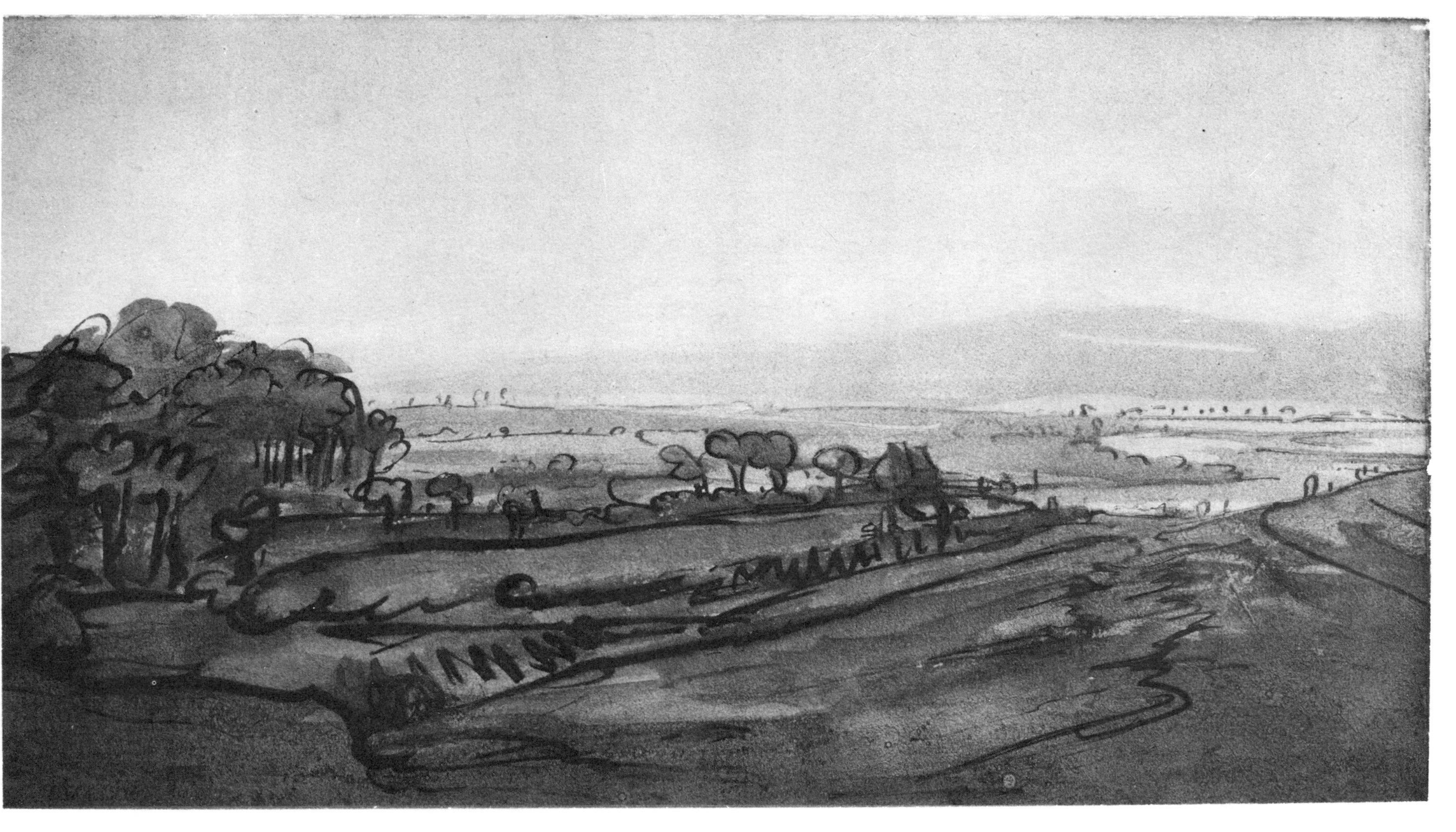

10. View in Gelderland. Ca. 1648. Pen and brush, wash, in bistre. 145 x 261 mm.
Comtesse de Béhague Collection, Paris.

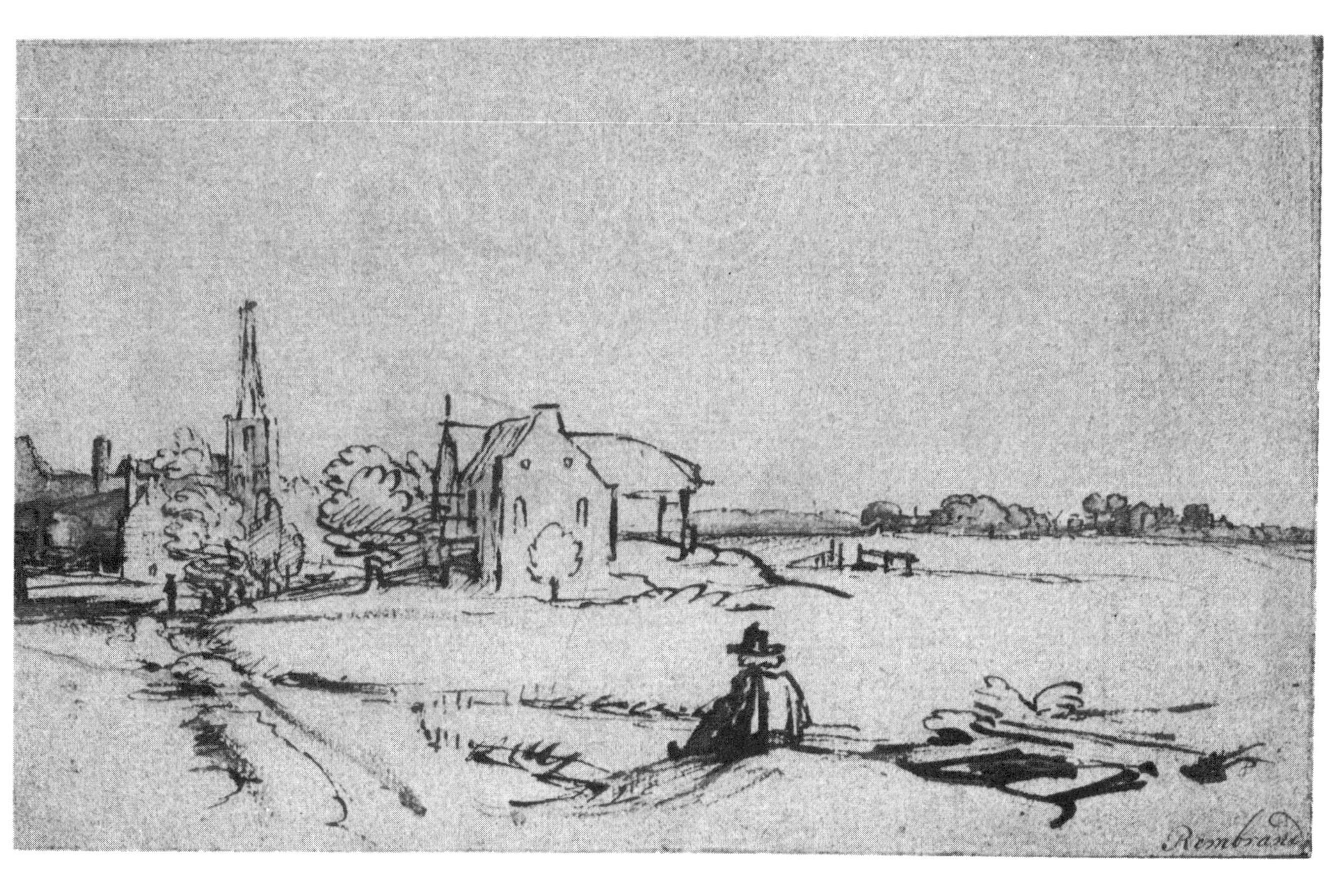

11. View of Diemen. Ca. 1648. Pen and bistre, wash. 112 x 175 mm. V. de Stuers Collection, The Hague.

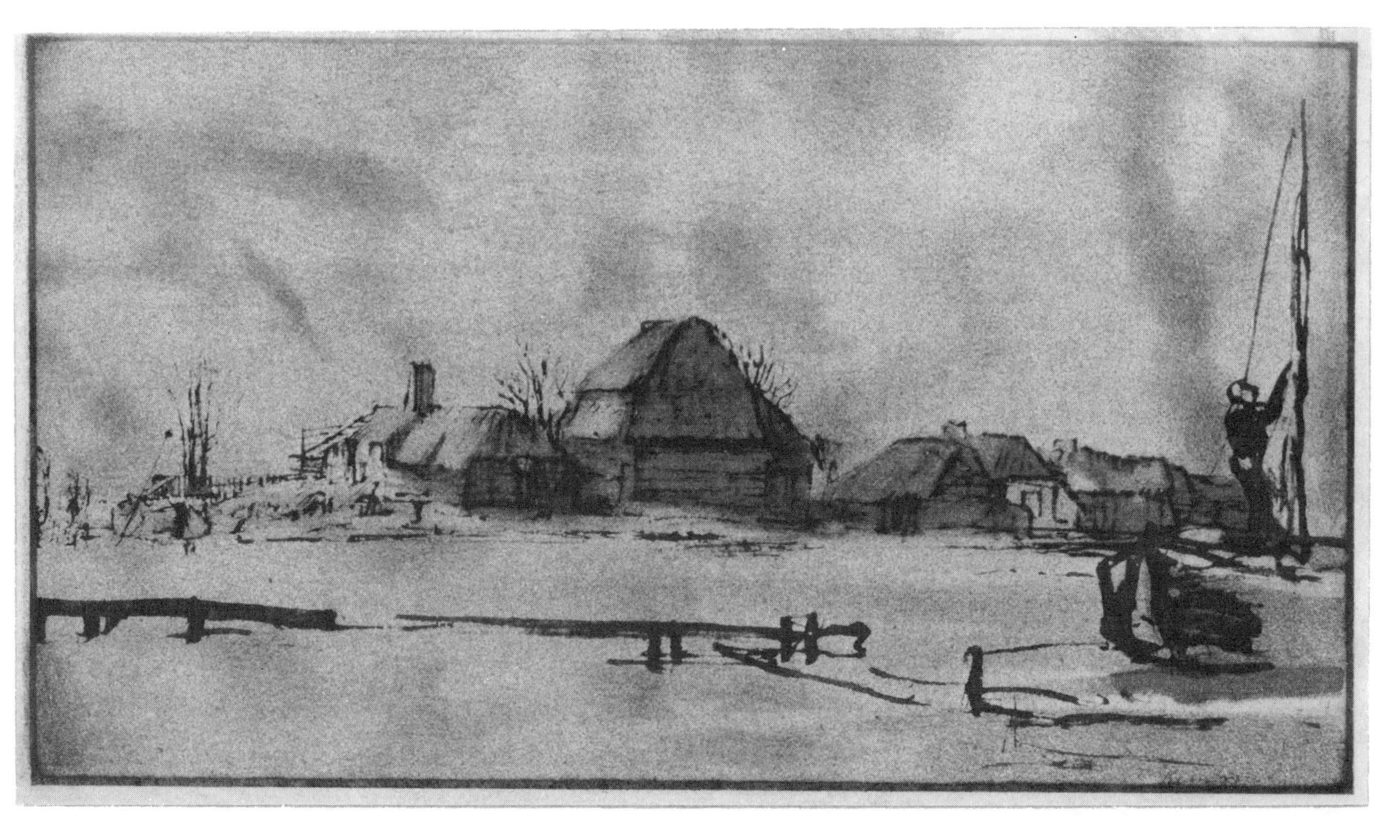

12. WINTER LANDSCAPE WITH A FARM. Ca. 1648–50. Pen and washes in bistre, Indian ink. 103 x 180 mm. Rijksprentenkabinet, Amsterdam.

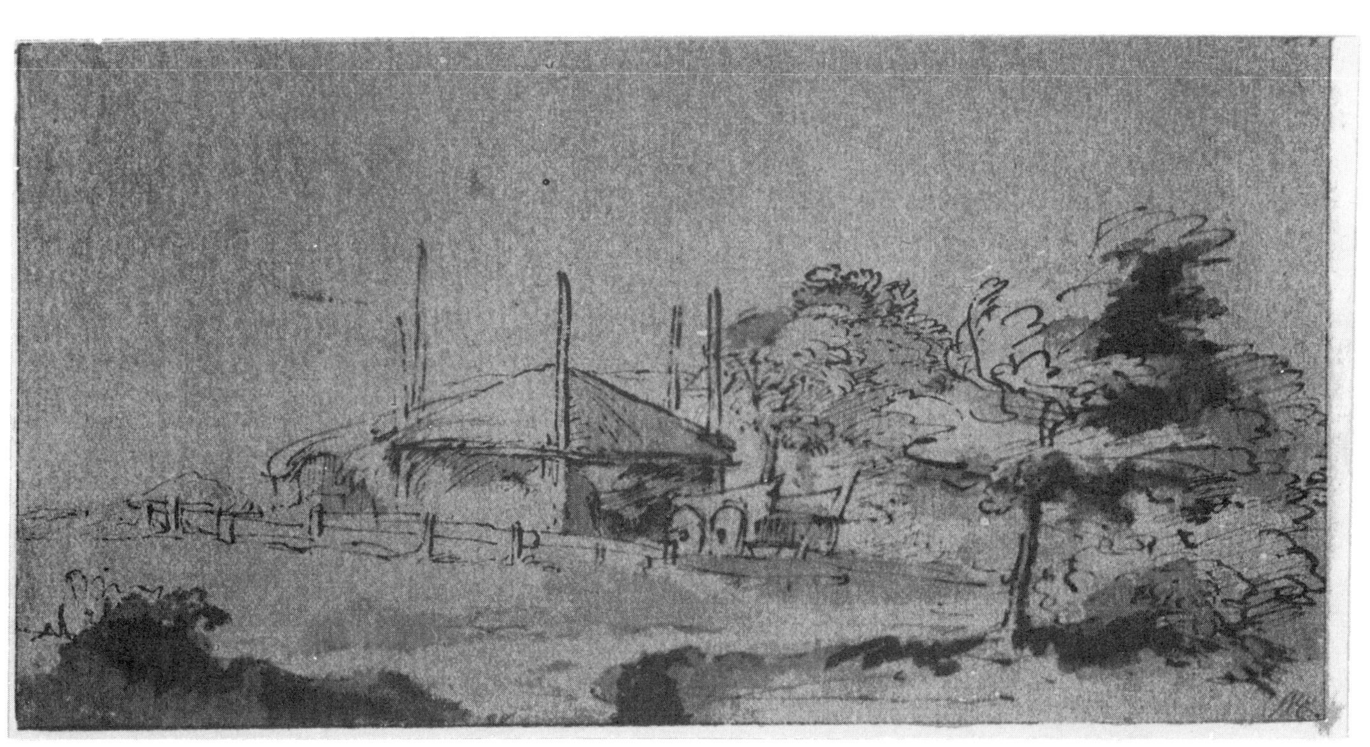

13. A FARM AMIDST TREES. Ca. 1648–40. Pen and wash in bistre on paper tinted brown. 95 x 176 mm. Rijksprentenkabinet, Amsterdam.

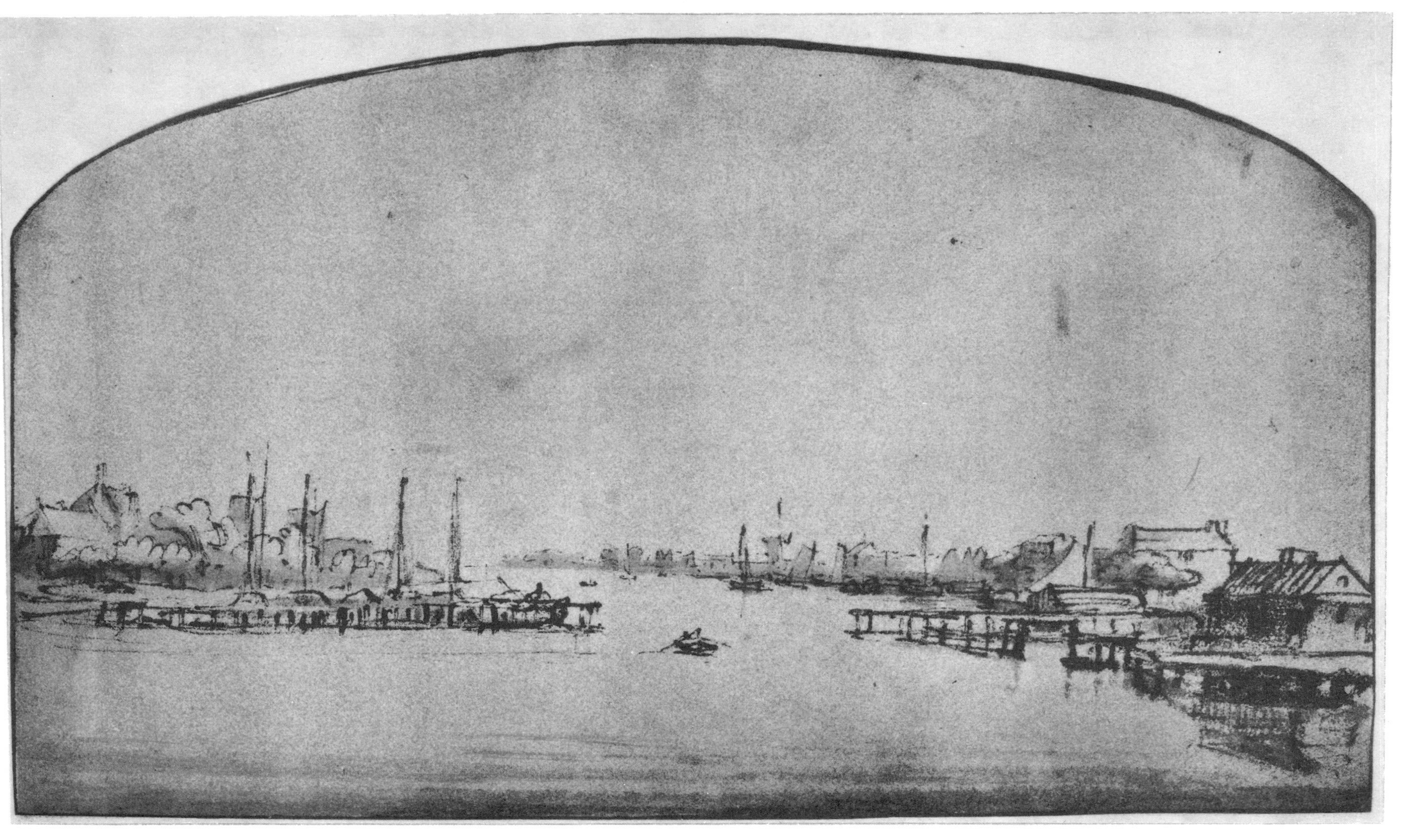

14. View Over the Amstel from the Blauwbrug in Amsterdam. Ca. 1648–50. Pen and wash on vellum. 132 x 232 mm. Rijksprentenkabinet, Amsterdam.

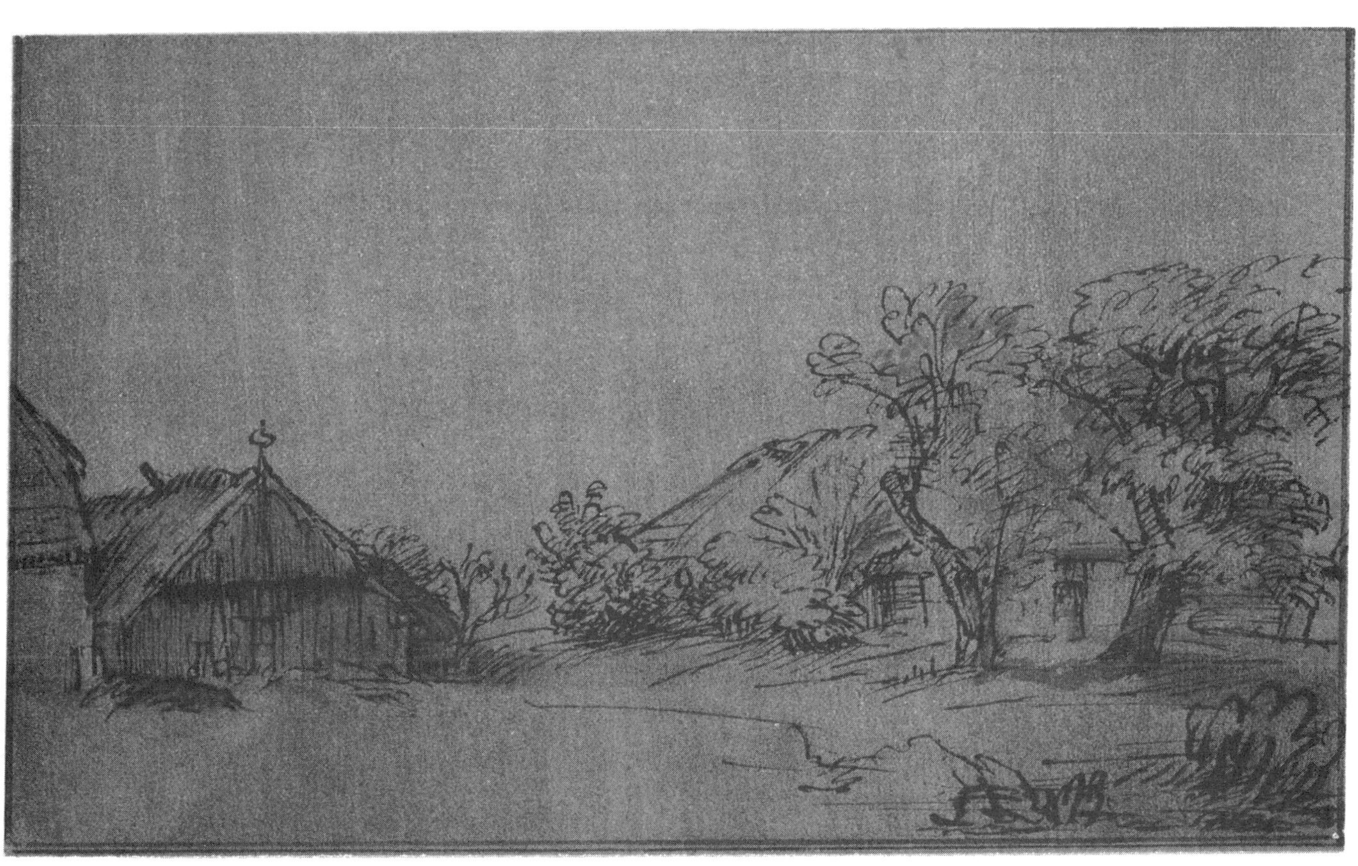

15. Farmhouses with Trees on the Right. Ca. 1648–50. Pen and bistre on brownish paper. 110 x 178 mm. Kupferstichkabinett, Berlin.

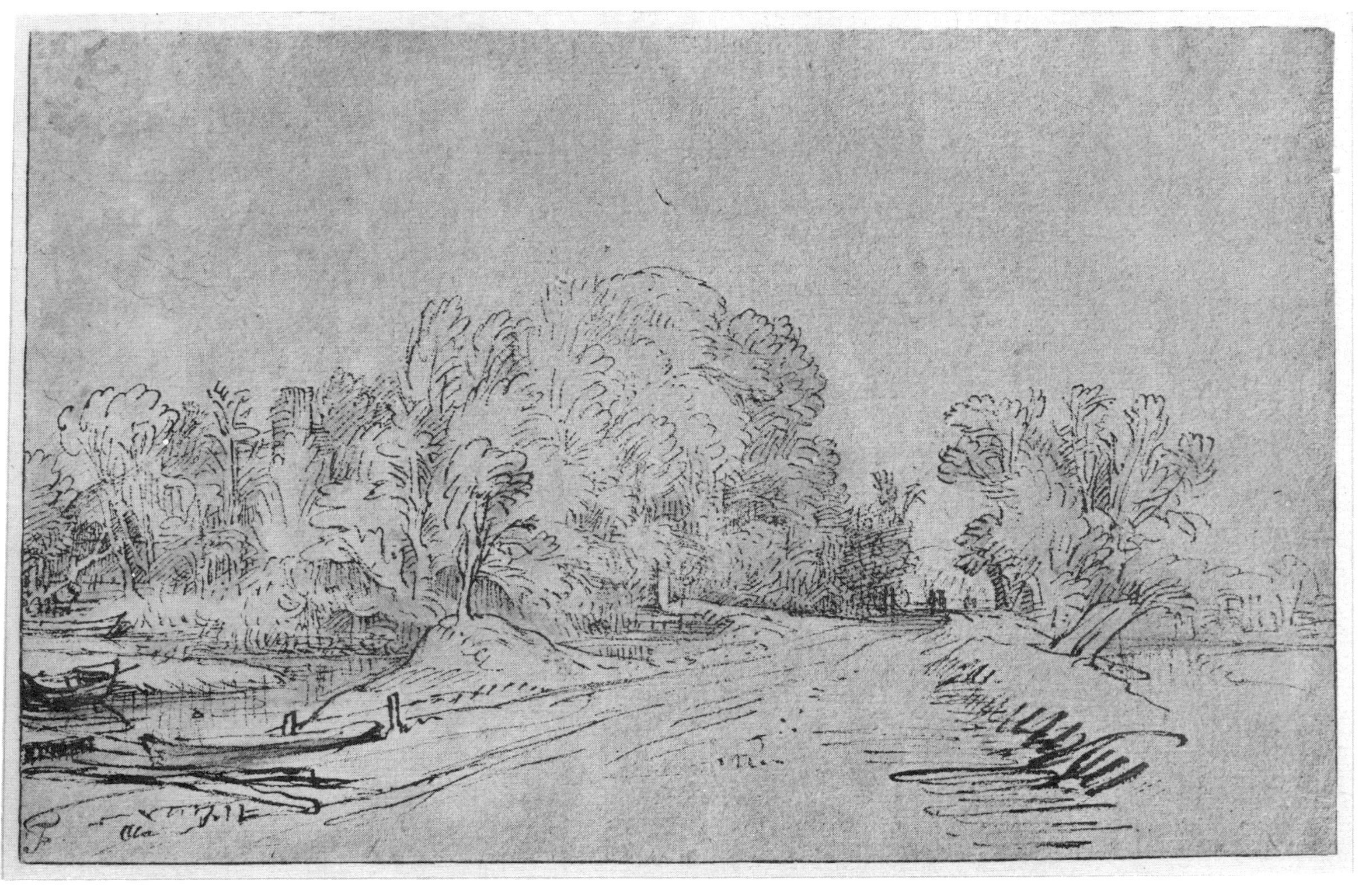

16. A Canal Near a Road with a Group of Trees in the Background. Ca. 1650. Pen and bistre, wash. 127 x 200 mm. Chatsworth Settlement.

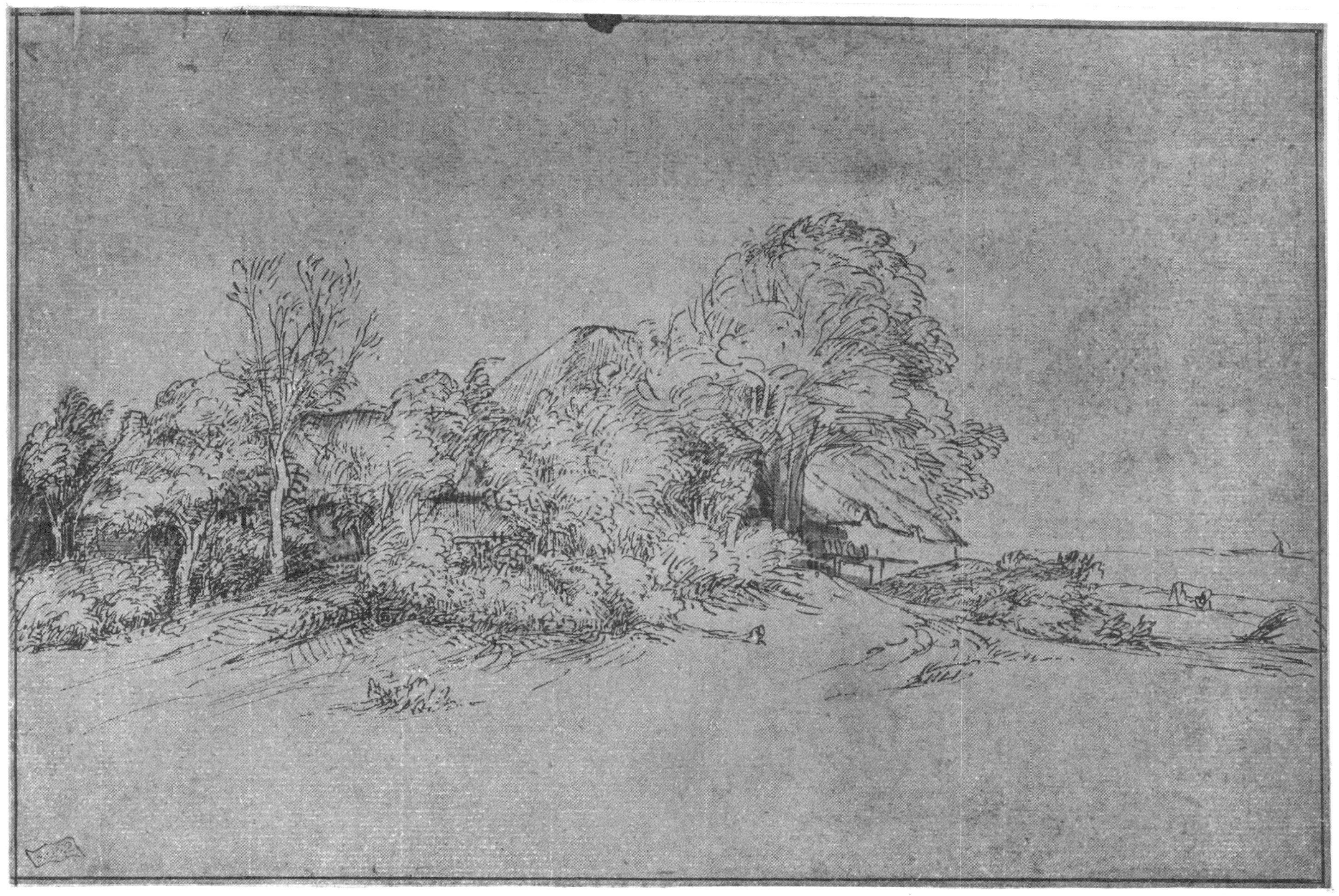

17. FARMHOUSES WITH A WATER MILL AMIDST TREES. Ca. 1650. Pen and bistre, wash. 158 x 240 mm. Museum, Groningen.

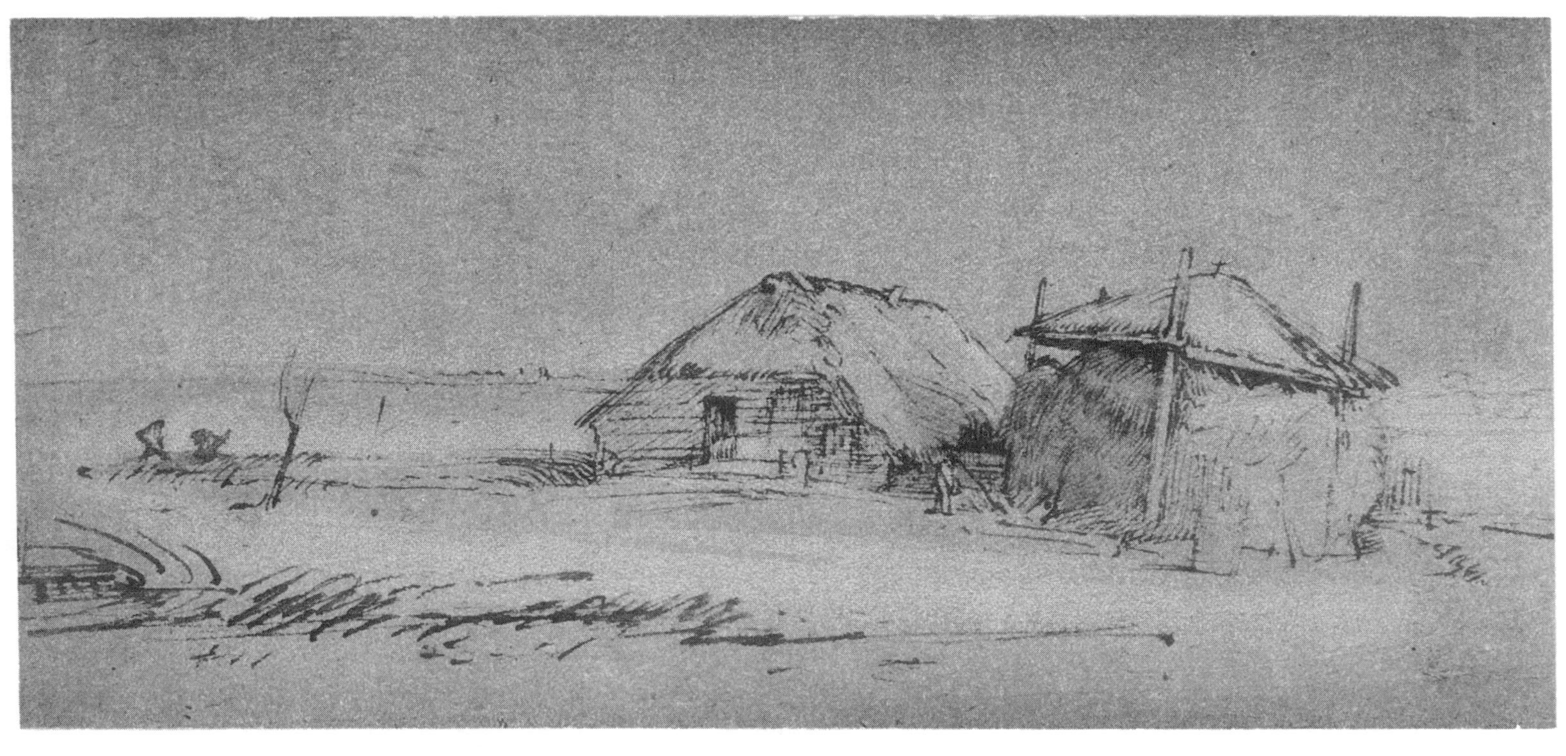

18. LANDSCAPE WITH A FARMER'S HOUSE AND A HAYRICK. Ca. 1650. Pen and bistre. 98 x 208 mm. Rijksprentenkabinet, Amsterdam.

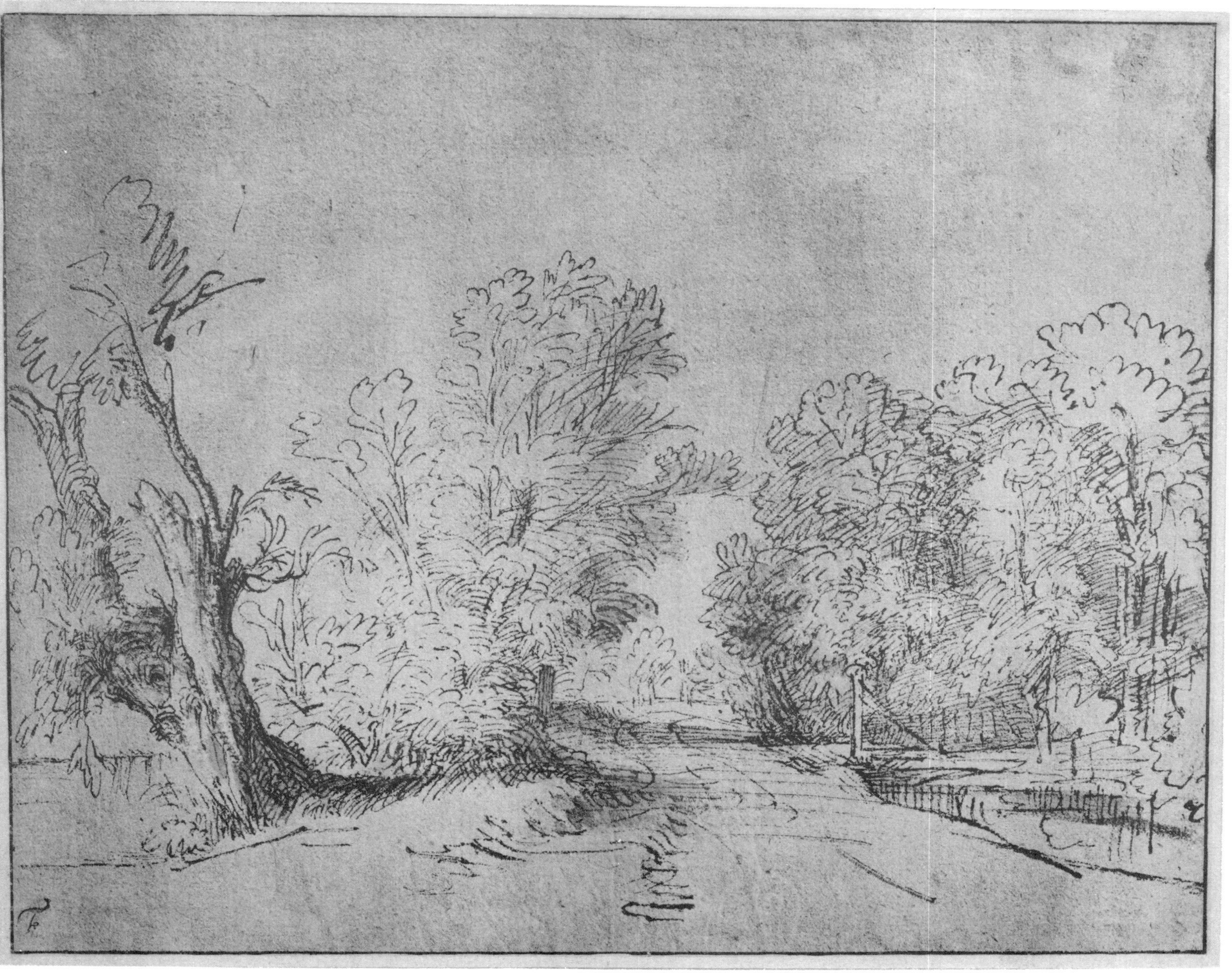

19. A Road Through a Wood. Ca. 1650. Pen and bistre, wash. 156 x 200 mm. Chatsworth Settlement.

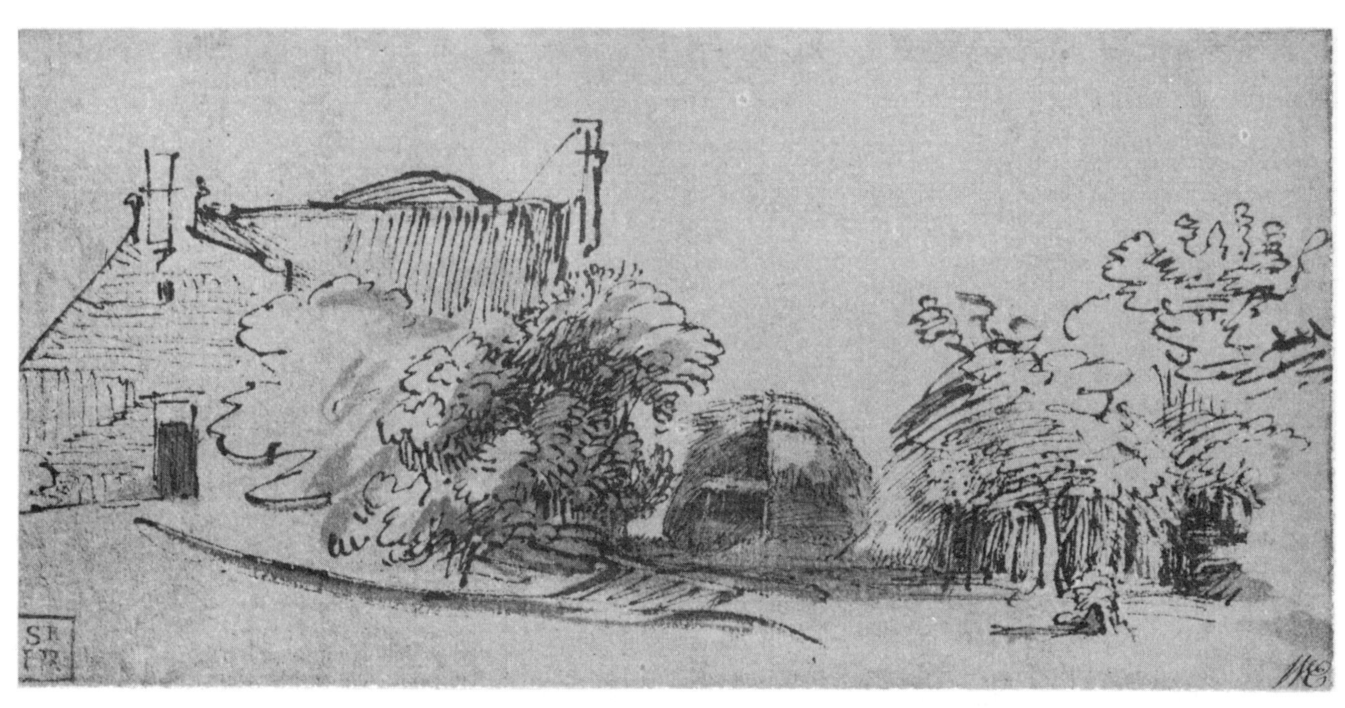

20. A Farmhouse with a Haystack Between Trees. Ca. 1650. Pen and bistre, wash in bistre and sepia. 89 x 179 mm. Boymans-van Beuningen Museum, Rotterdam.

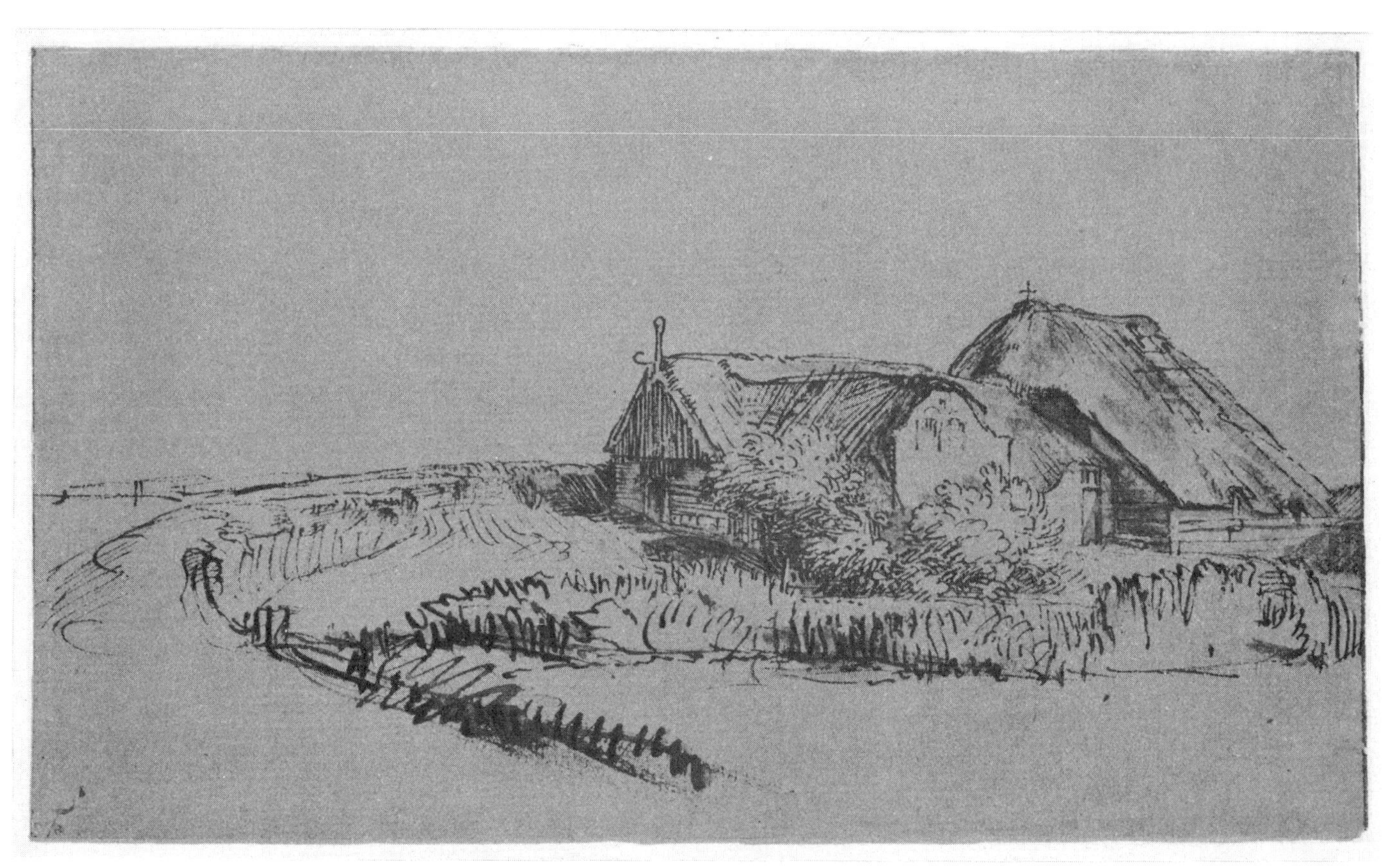

21. Farmstead at the Diemerdijk. Ca. 1650. Pen and bistre, wash. 127 x 212 mm. Chatsworth Settlement.

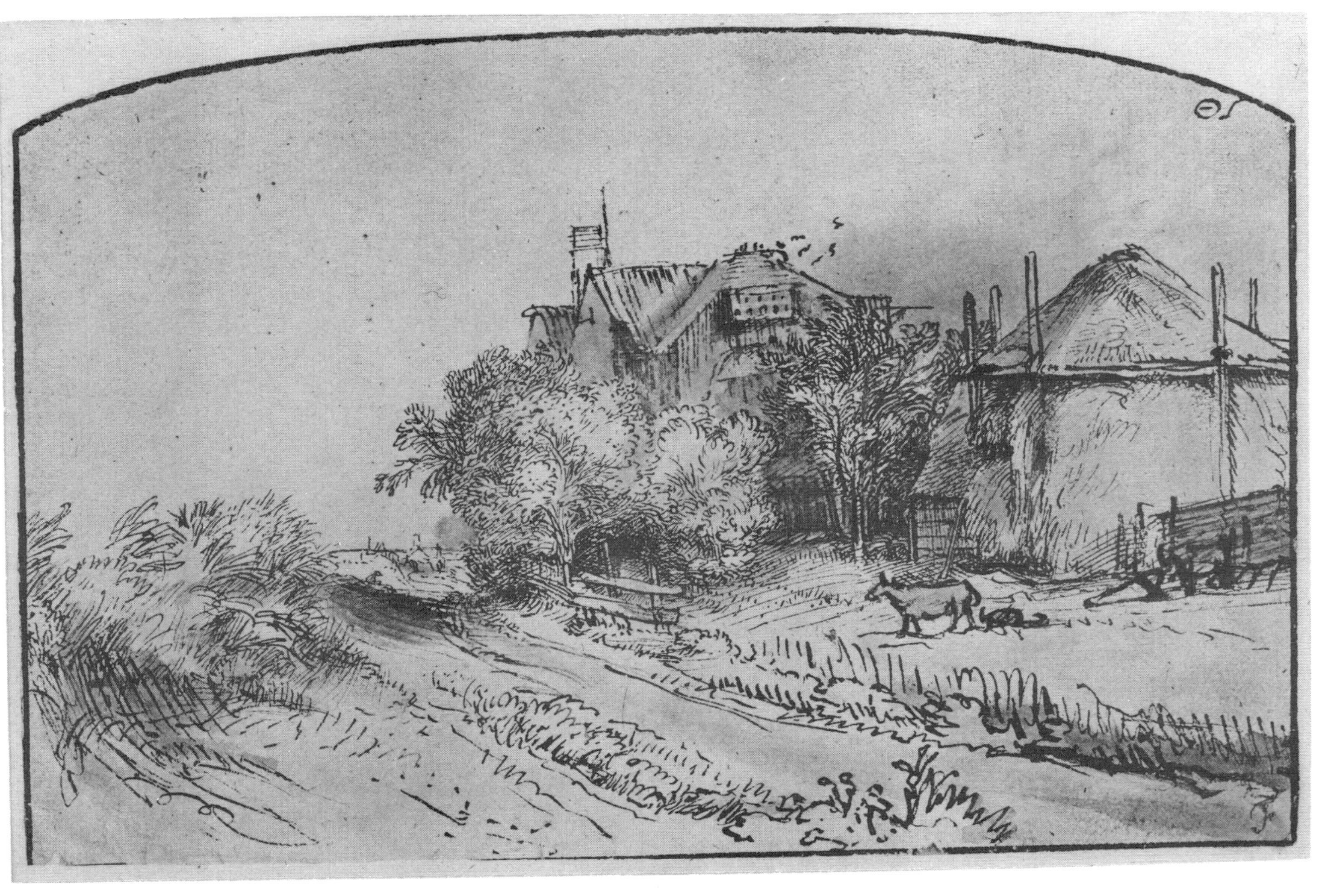

22. A Hayrick Near a Farm. Ca. 1650. Pen and bistre, wash. 128 x 200 mm. Chatsworth Settlement.

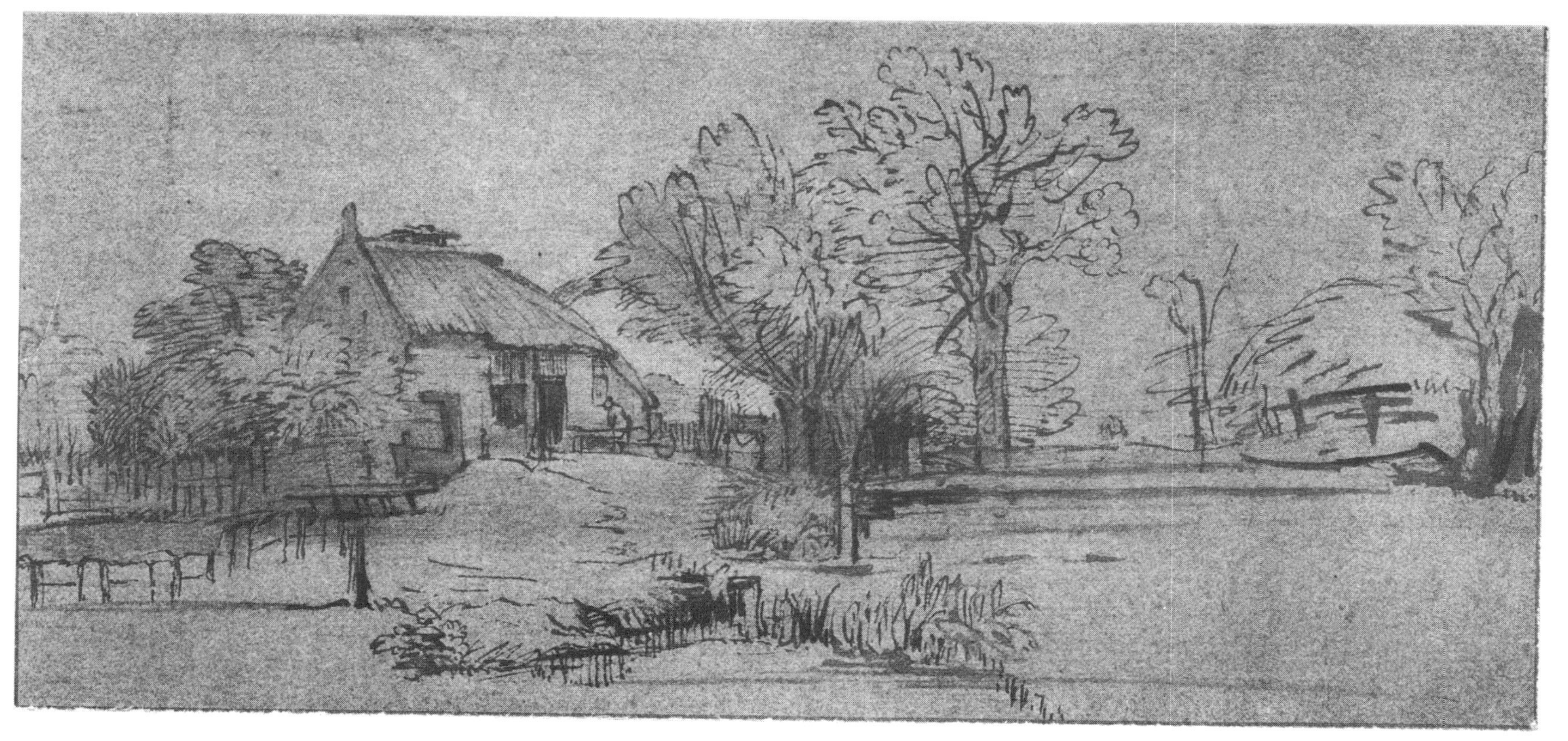

23. Cottages with Trees Beside Water and a Hay Barn. Ca. 1650. Pen and bistre, wash. 102 x 223 mm. British Museum, London.

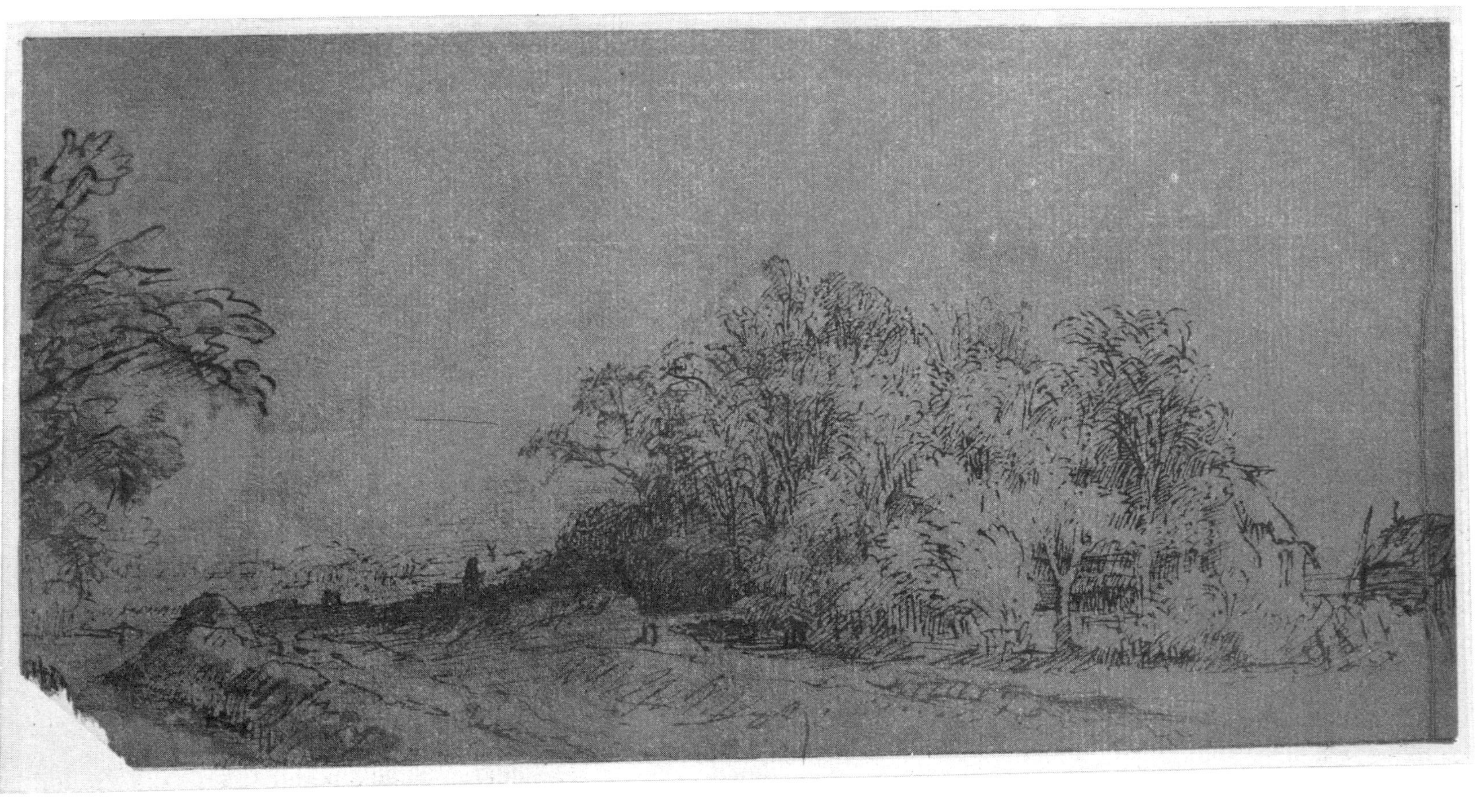

24. A Group of Trees and Huts Near a High Road. Ca. 1650. Pen and wash in bistre, some Indian ink wash. 110 x 219 mm. Chatsworth Settlement.

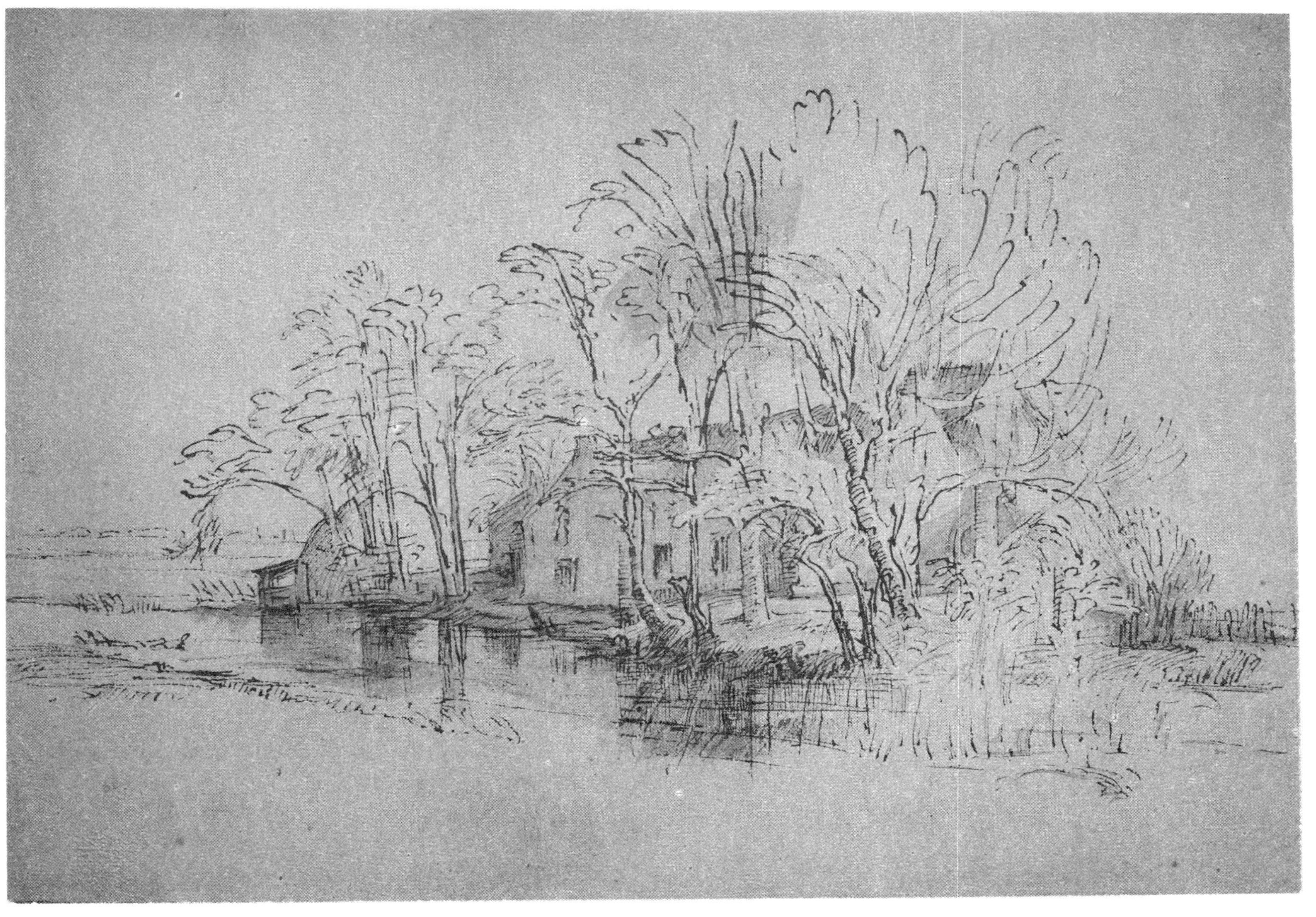

25. Houses Among Trees on the Bank of a River. Ca. 1650. Pen and wash in Indian ink. 160 x 233 mm. British Museum, London.

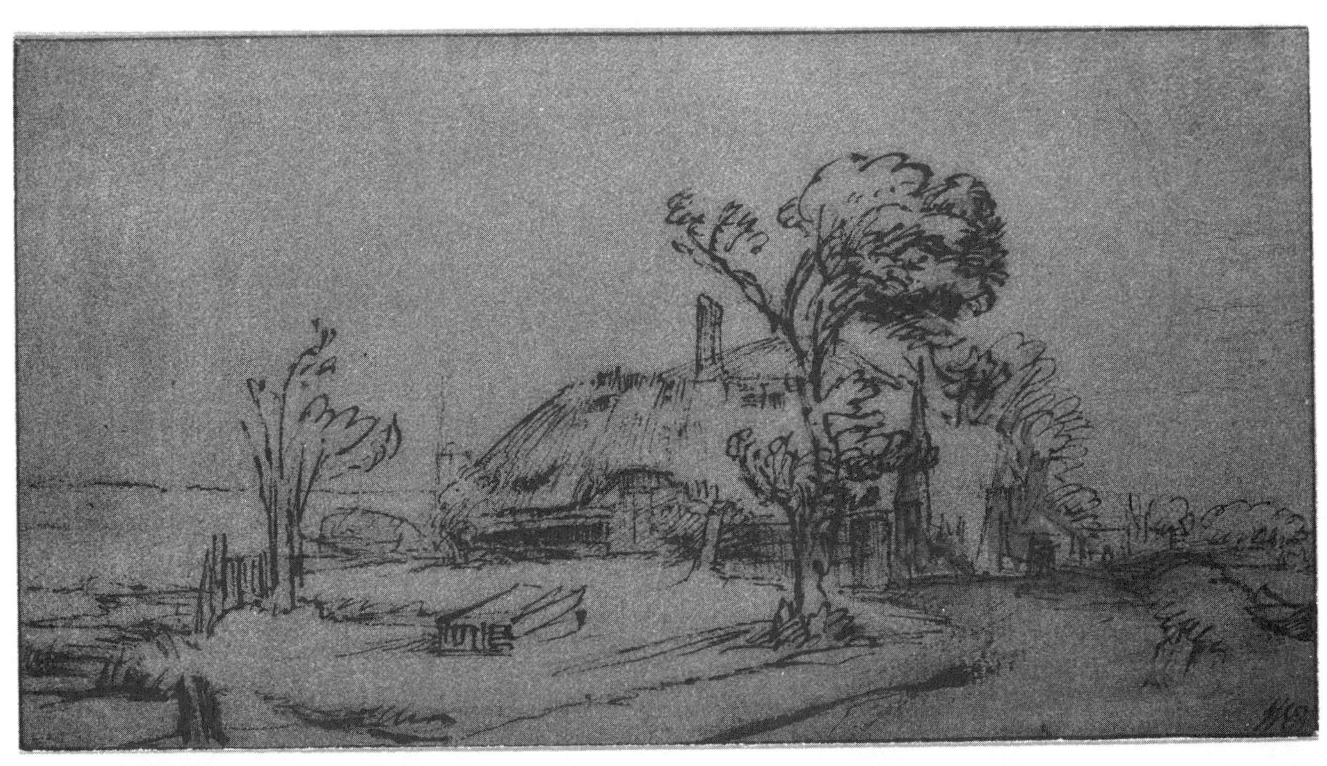

26. Landscape with Cottages at the Left Side of a Road. Ca. 1650. Pen and bistre in wash, on brownish paper. 94 x 172 mm. Kupferstichkabinett, Berlin.

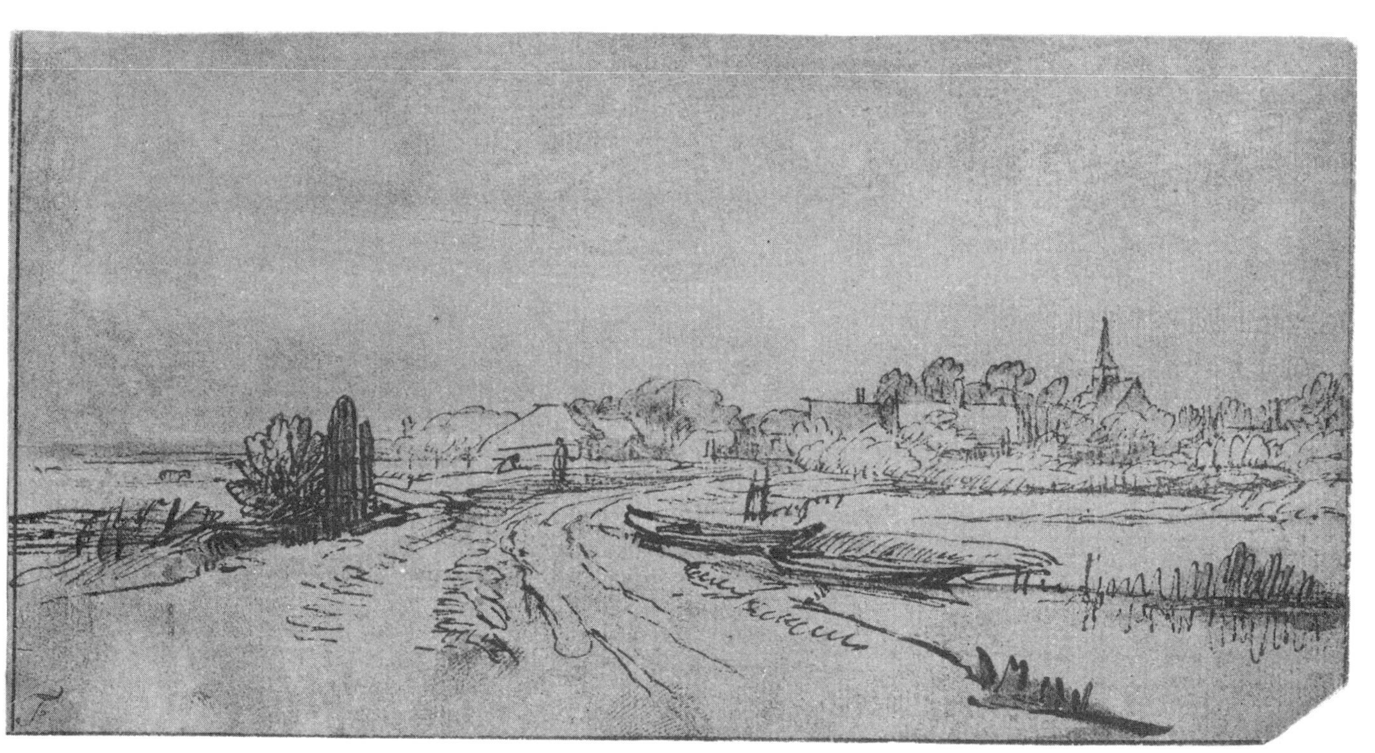

27. View of Sloten. Ca. 1650. Pen and bistre, wash, white body color, on brown prepared paper. 96 x 180 mm. Chatsworth Settlement.

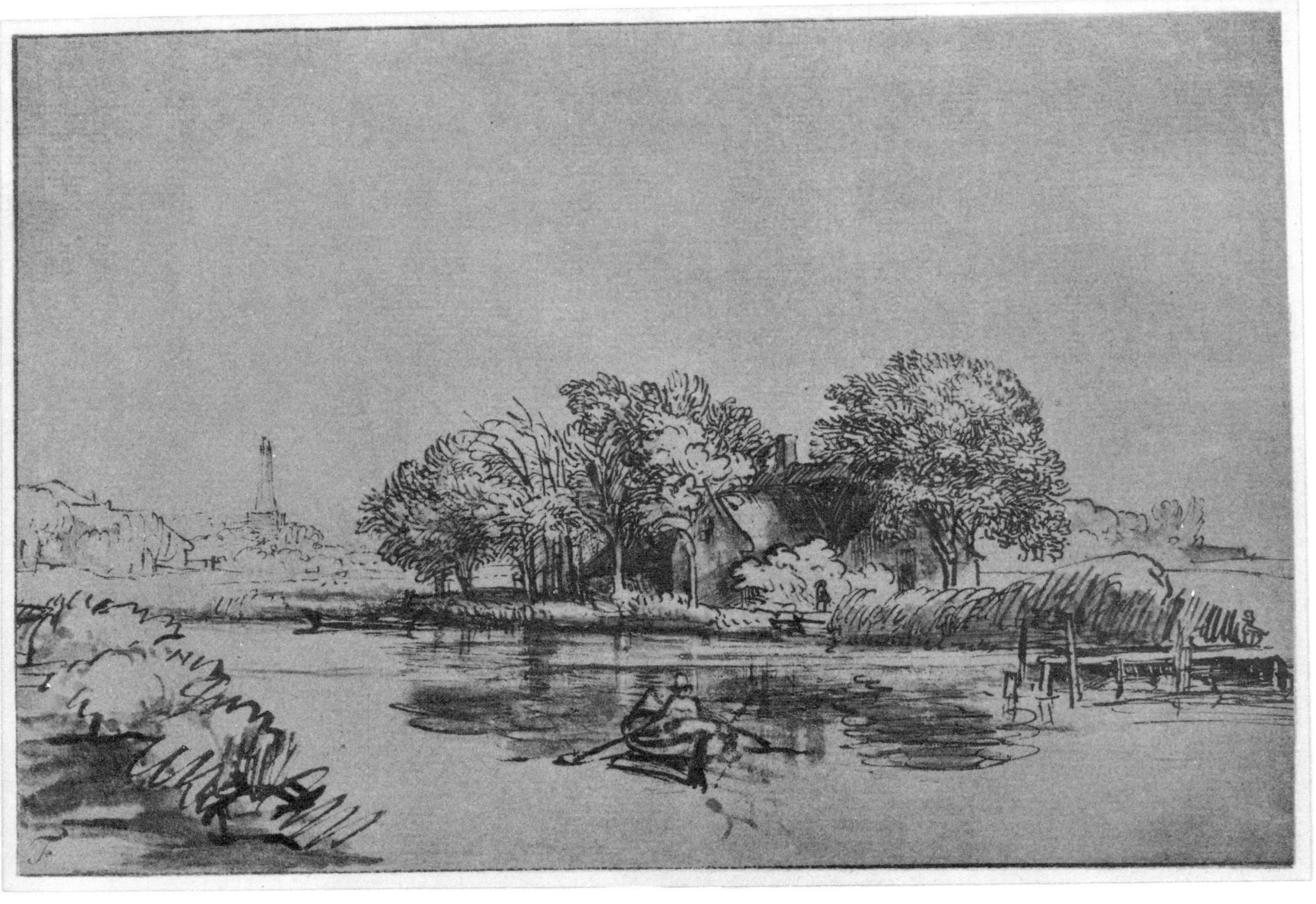

28. A Farmhouse Among Trees Beside a Canal with a Man in a Rowboat. Ca. 1650. Pen and bistre, wash, white body color. 133 x 204 mm. Chatsworth Settlement.

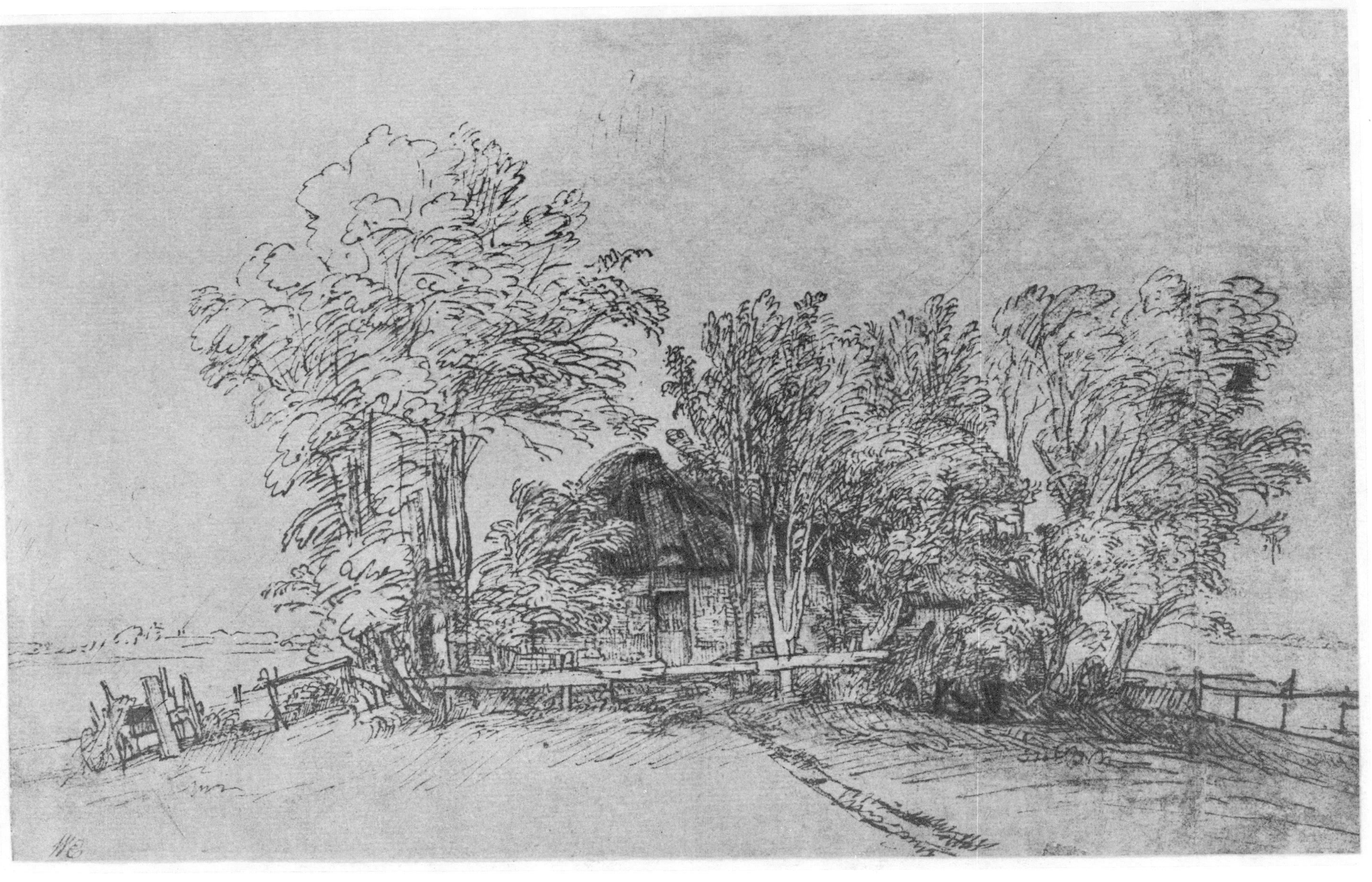

29. A Thatched Cottage Among Trees. Ca. 1650. Pen and bistre, wash. 172 x 271 mm. Metropolitan Museum of Art, New York.

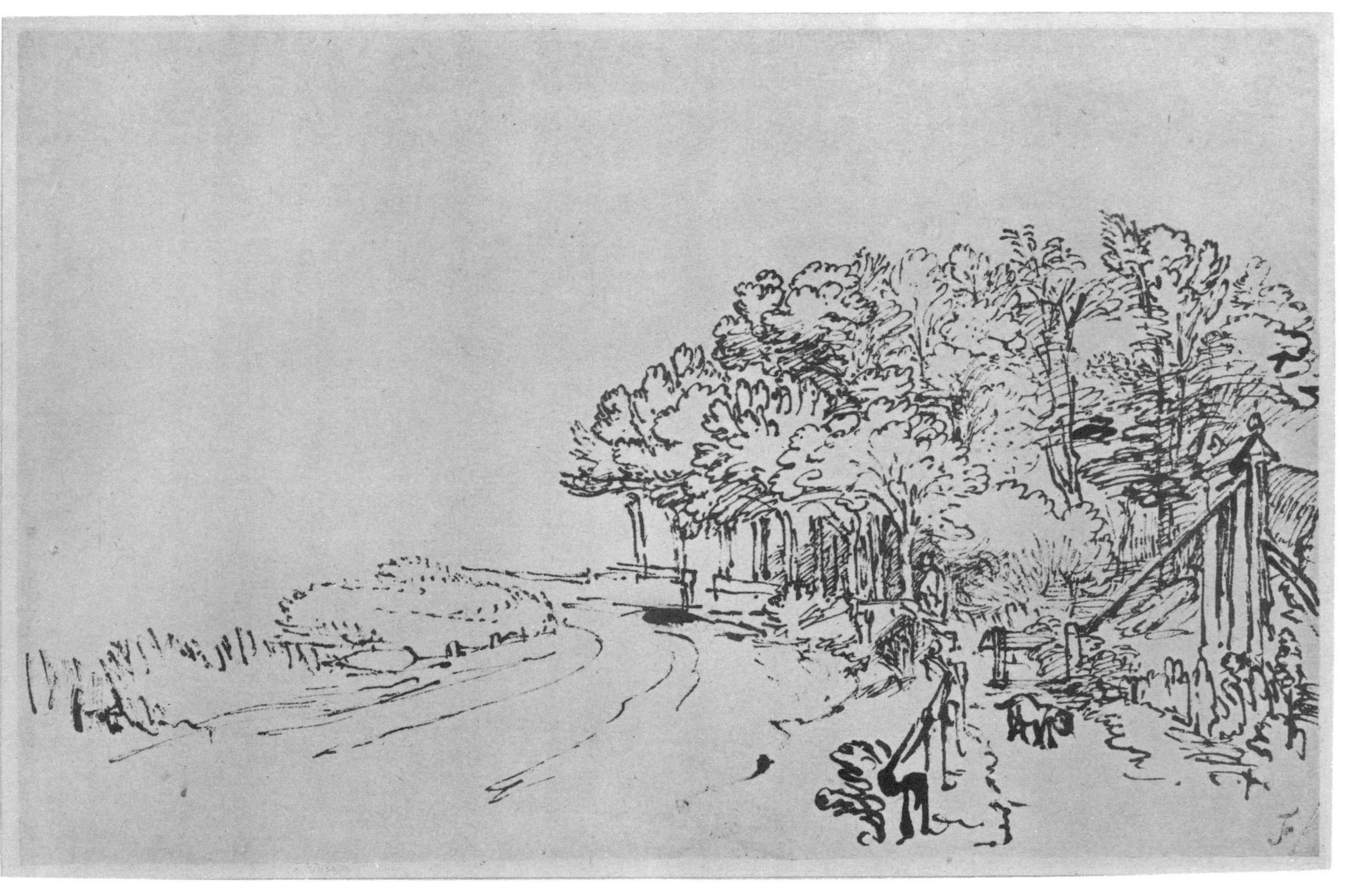

30. The Amsteldijk near the Trompenburg Estate. Ca. 1650. Pen and bistre. 132 x 207 mm. Chatsworth Settlement.

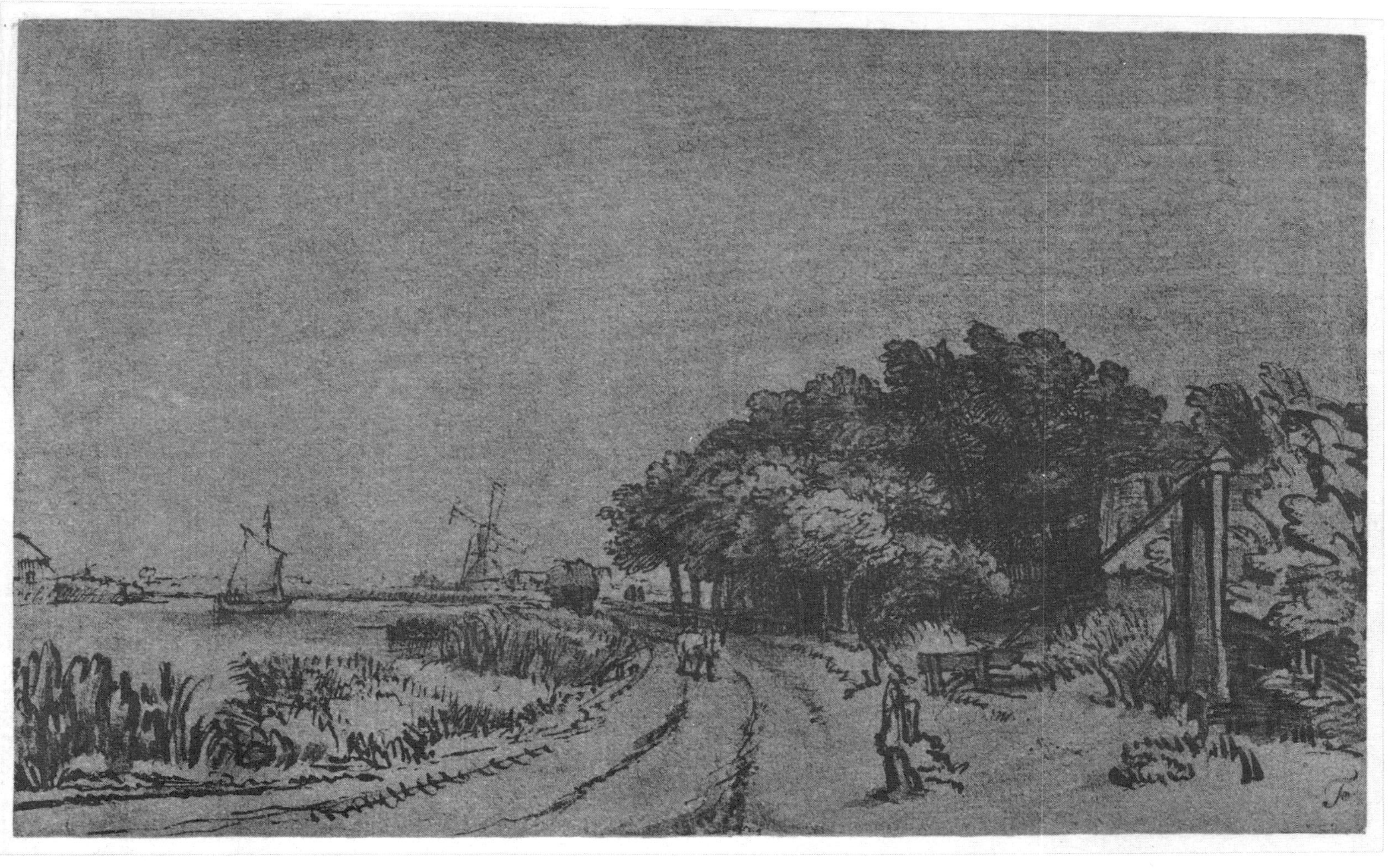

31. THE AMSTELDIJK NEAR THE TROMPENBURG ESTATE. Ca. 1650. Pen and wash in bistre, white body color, on brown prepared paper. 130 x 217 mm. Chatsworth Settlement.

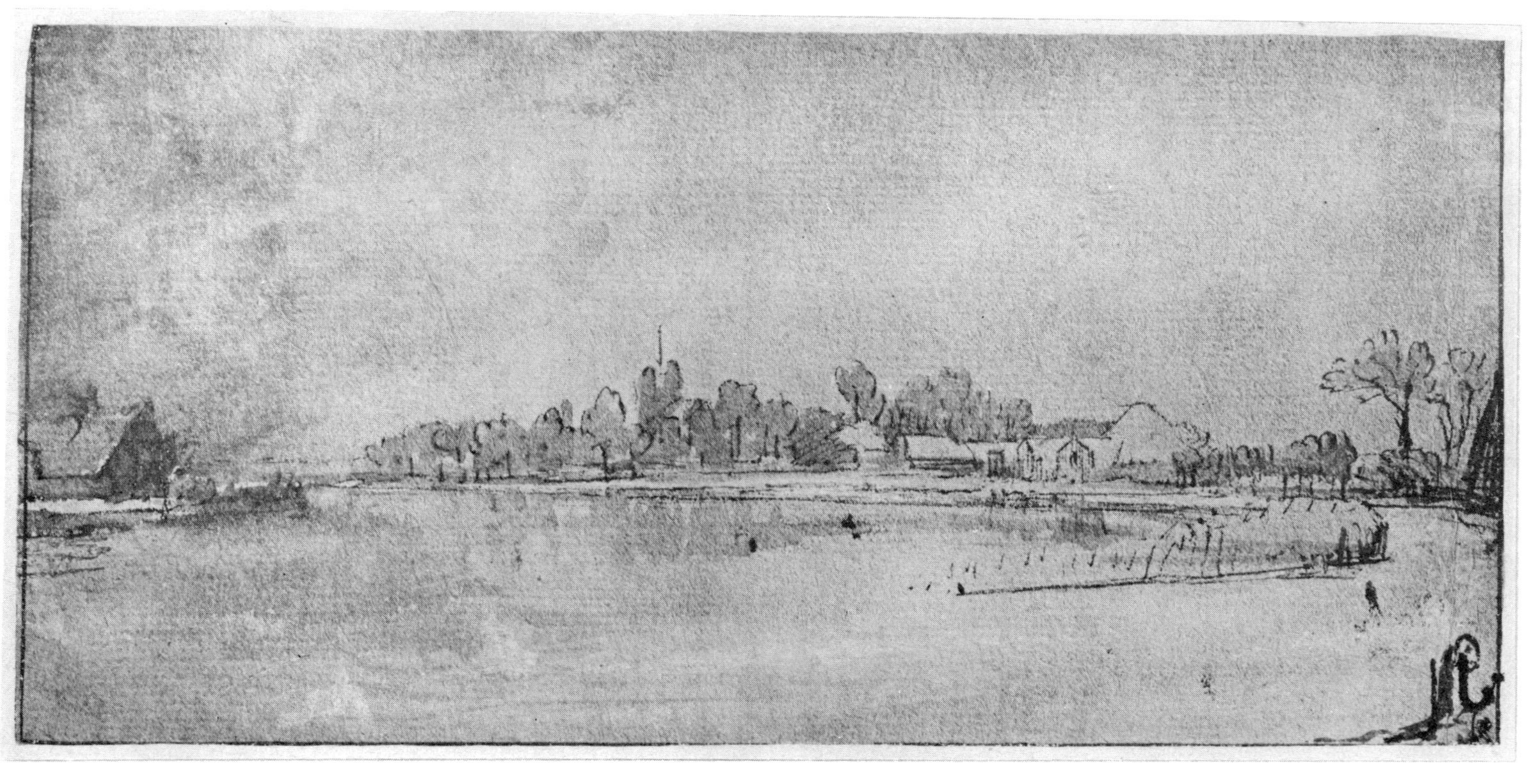

32. The Bend of the Amstel River Near Kostverloren Castle. Ca. 1650. Pen and bistre, wash, white body color. 97 x 199 mm. Chatsworth Settlement.

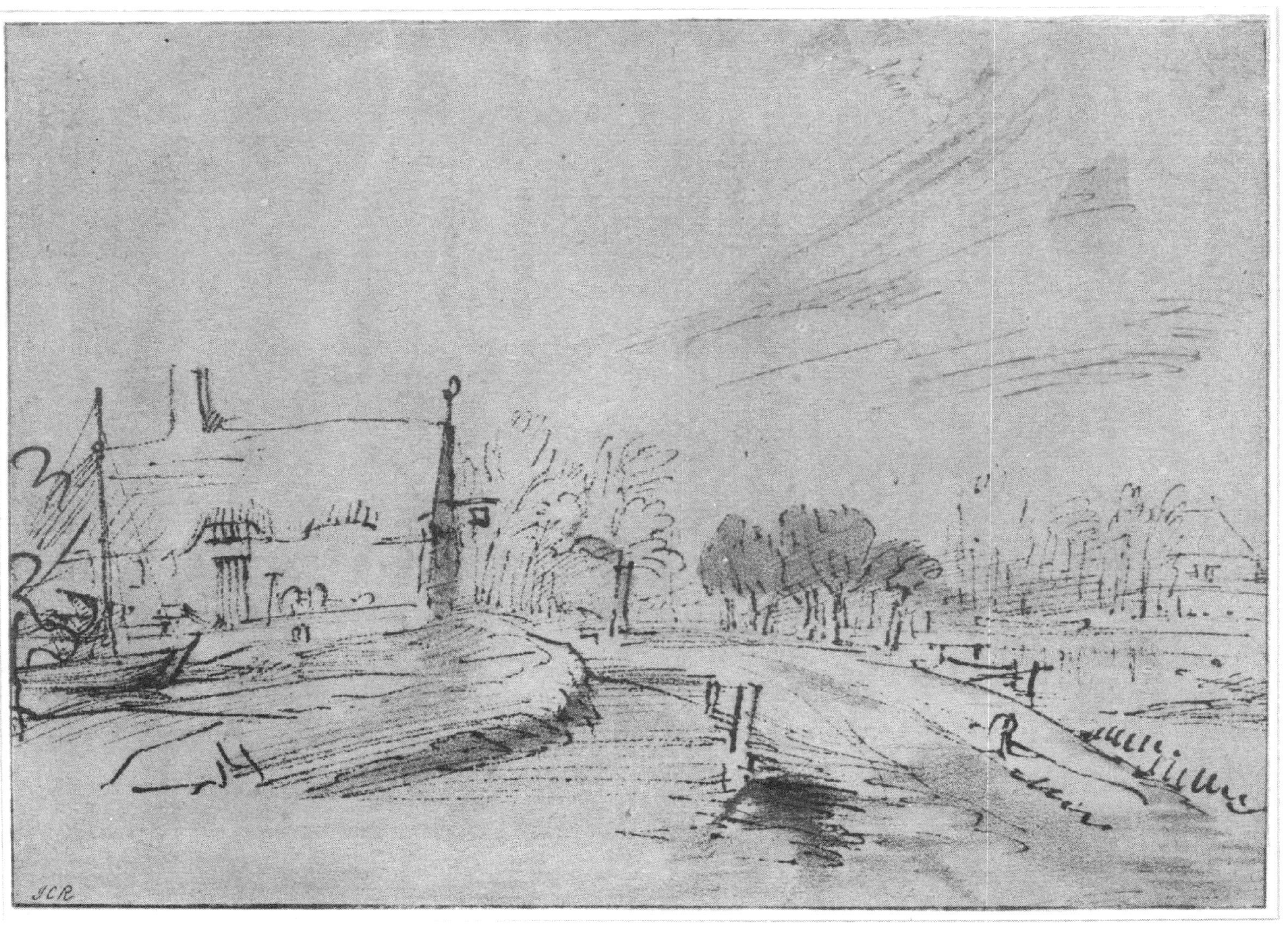

33. Landscape with an Inn, and a Sailboat on the Right. Ca. 1650. Pen and bistre, wash with Indian ink, on brownish paper. 140 x 190 mm. Rijksprentenkabinet, Amsterdam.

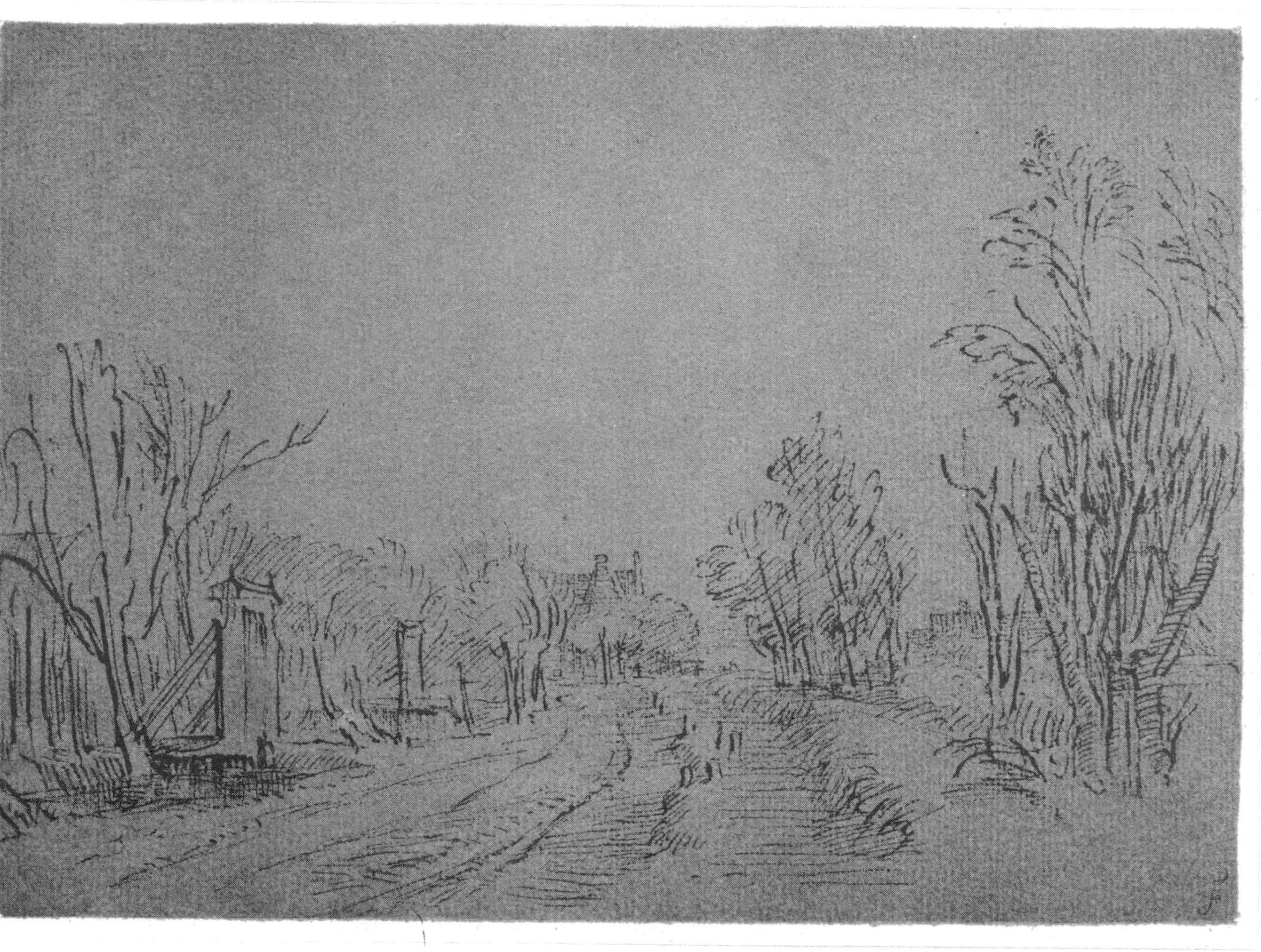

34. Village Street Beside a Canal. Ca. 1650. Pen and bistre. 133 x 184 mm. Chatsworth Settlement.

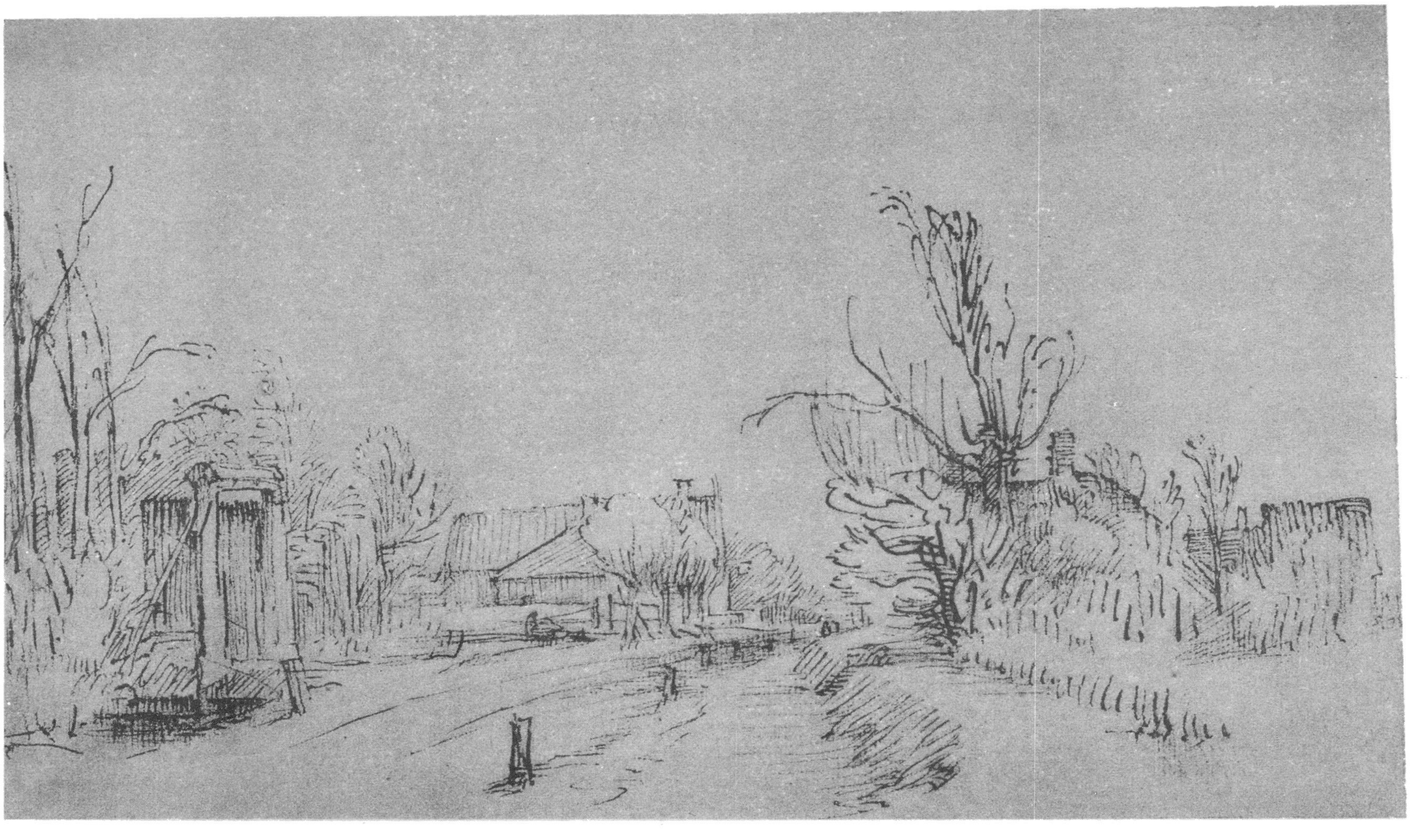

35. Village Street Beside a Canal. Ca. 1650. Pen and bistre. 130 x 231 mm. British Museum, London.

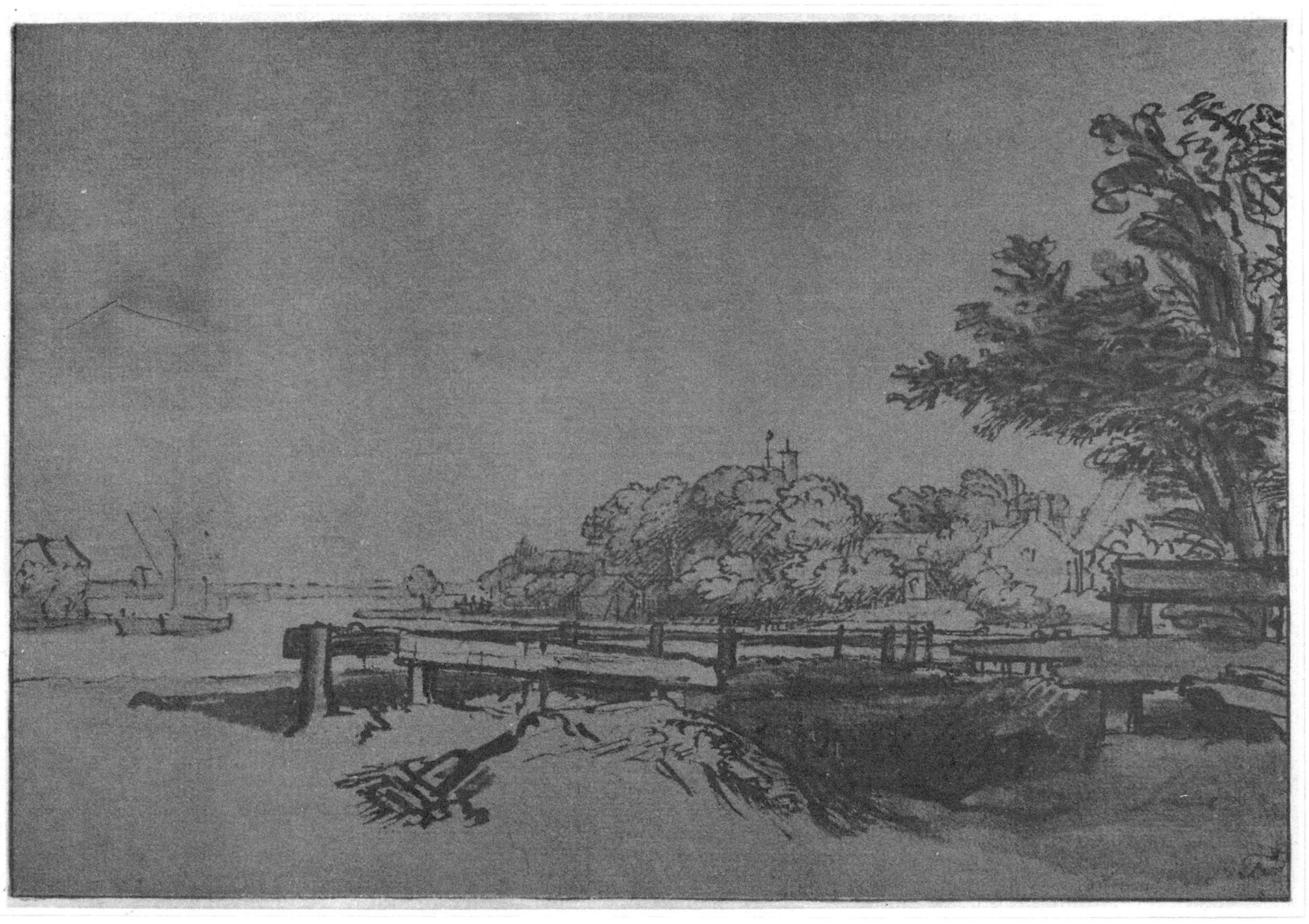

36. The Bend in the Amstel River, with Kostverloren Castle and a Fence in the Foreground. Ca. 1650. Reed pen and wash in bistre, white body color, on reddish brown prepared paper. 145 x 212 mm. Chatsworth Settlement.

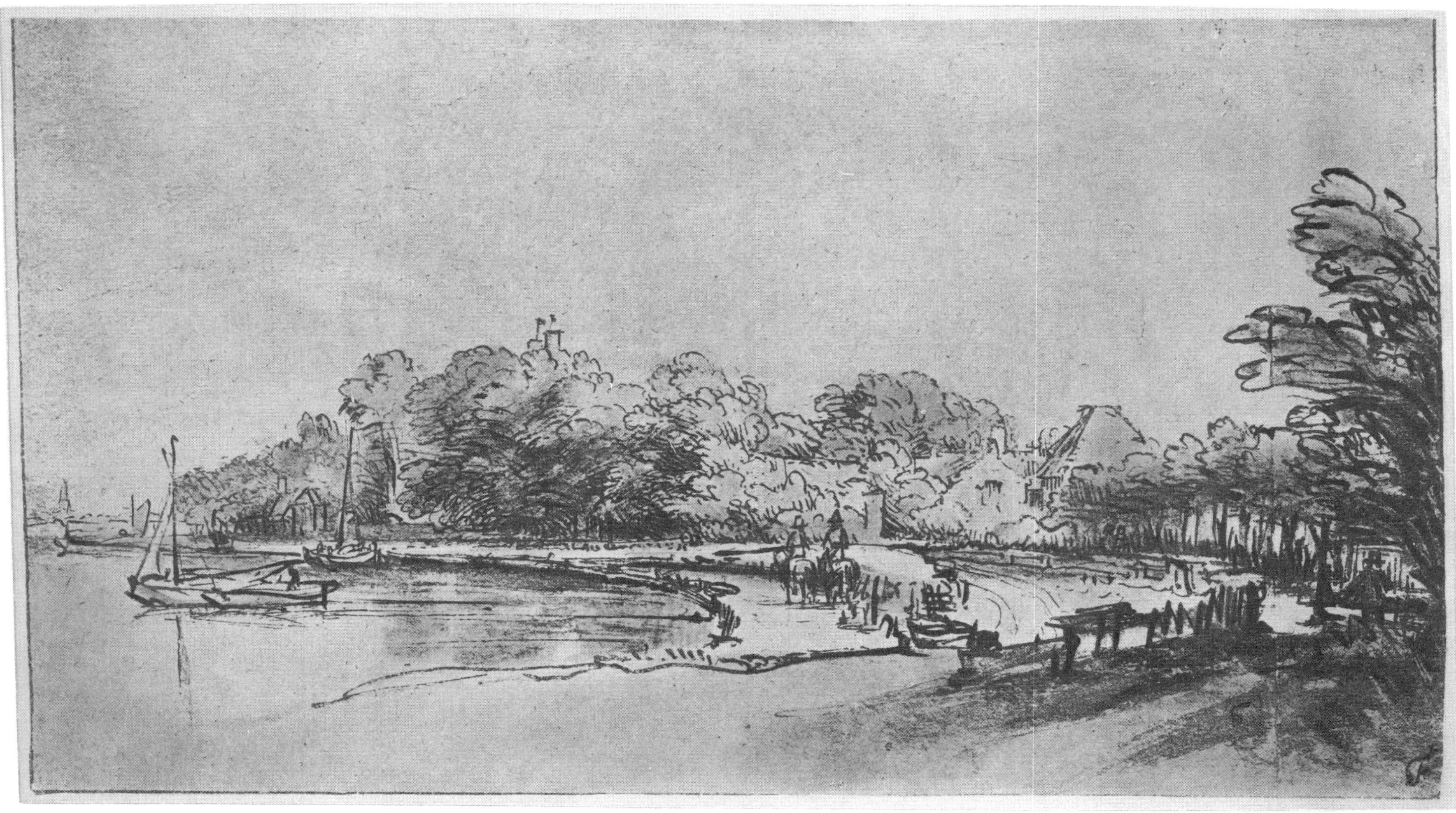

37. The Bend in the Amstel River, with Kostverloren Castle and Two Men on Horseback. Ca. 1650–52. Reed pen and brush in bistre, washes in bistre and Indian ink, white body color. 136 x 250 mm. Chatsworth Settlement.

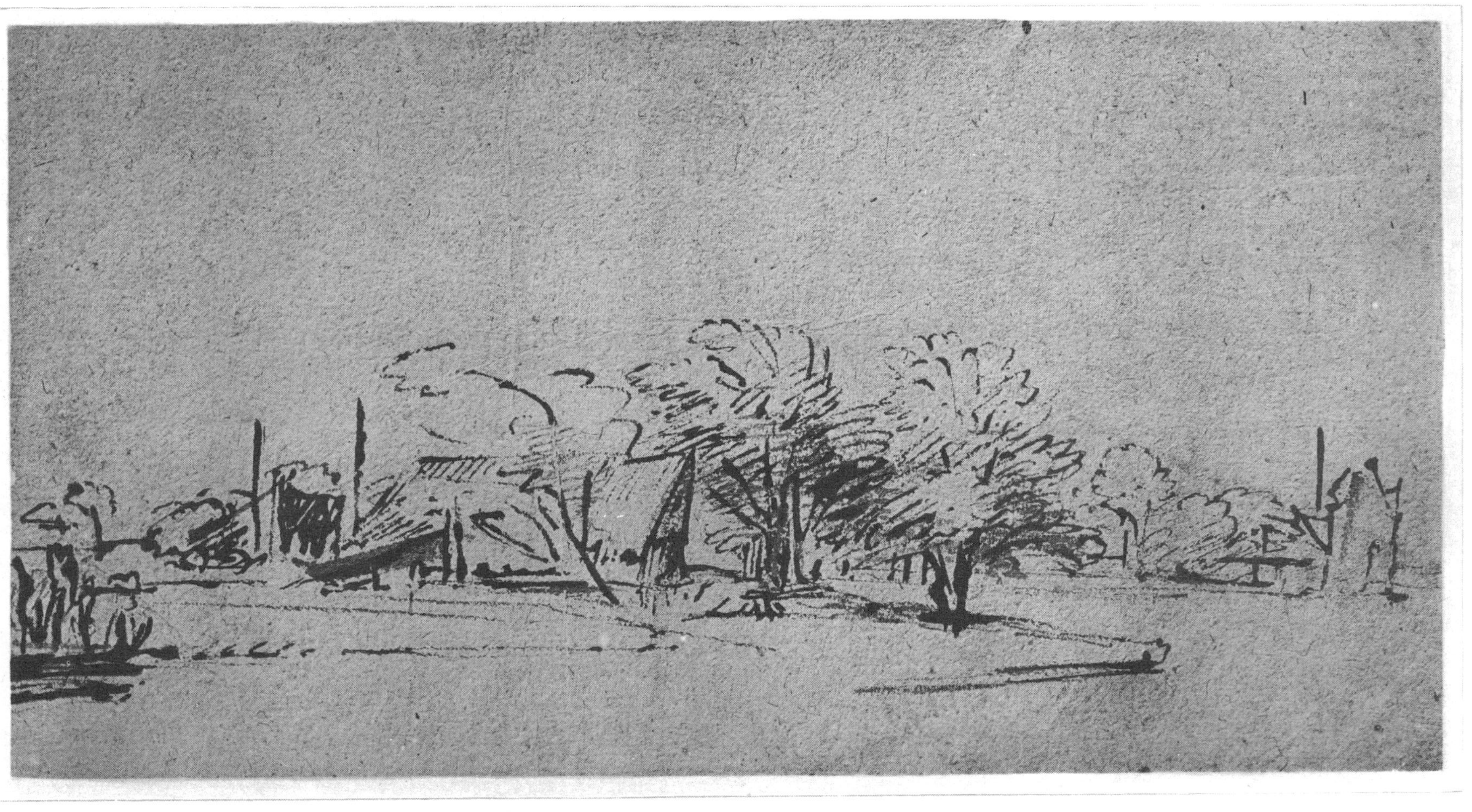

38. Farm Amidst Trees. Ca. 1650–53. Pen and bistre. 120 x 226 mm. Boymans-van Beuningen Museum, Rotterdam.

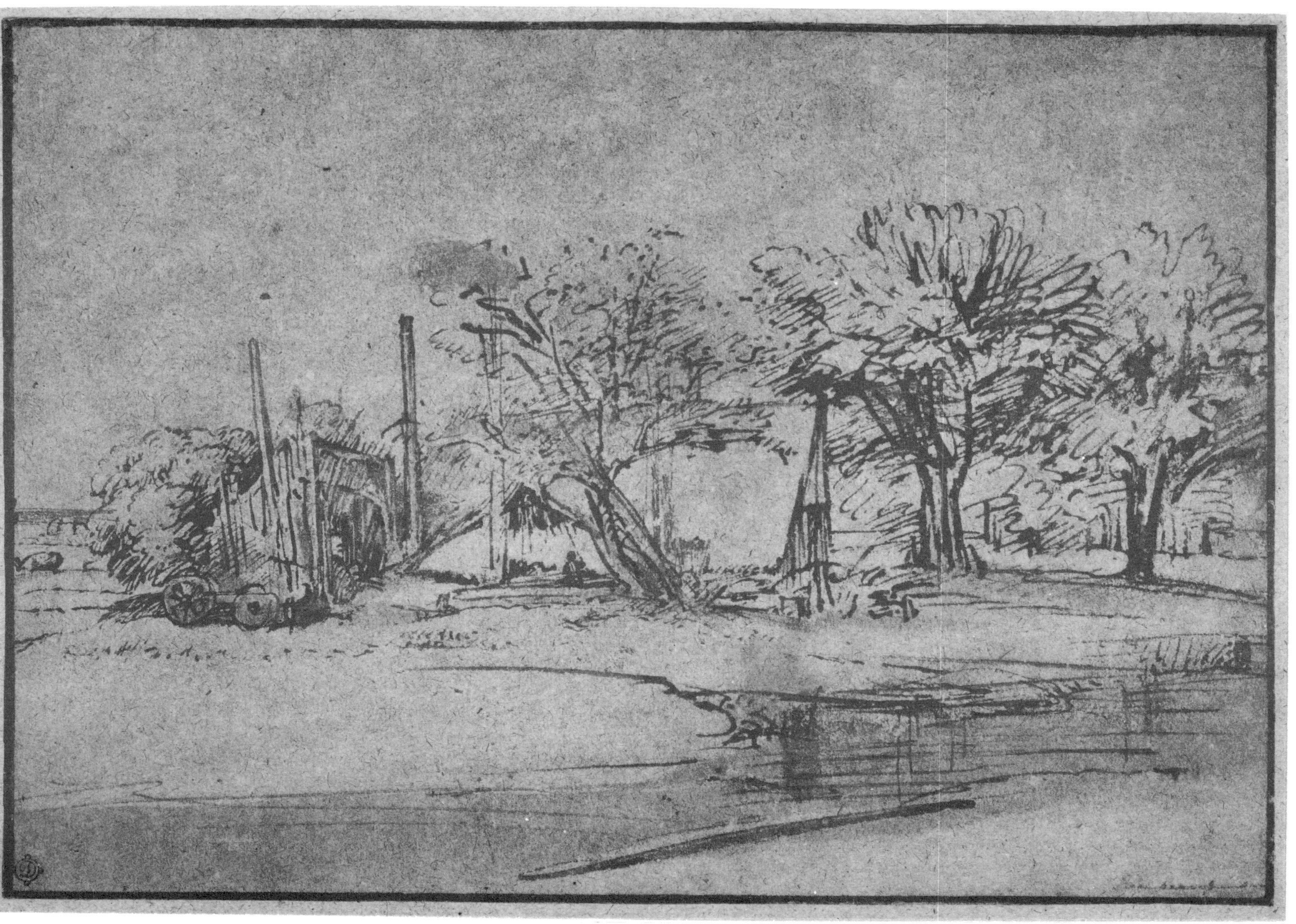

39. Farm Amidst Trees. Ca. 1650–53. Reed pen and wash in bistre. 156 x 226 mm. Frick Collection, New York.

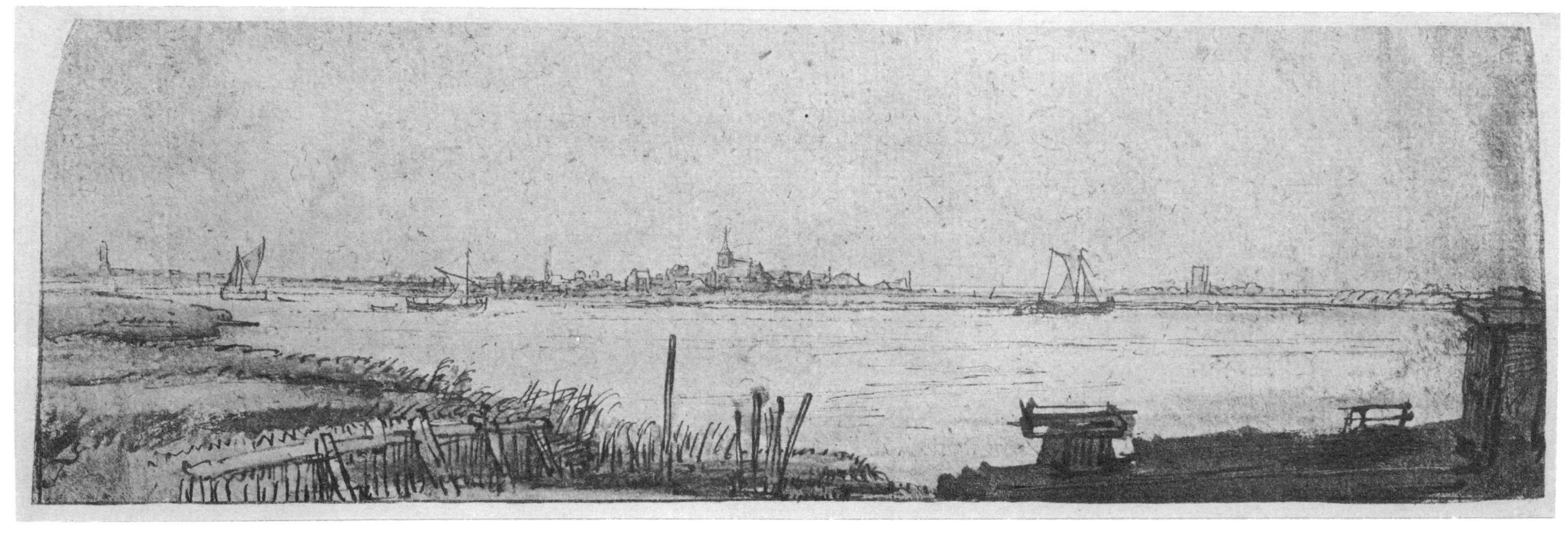

40. View Over "Het IJ" from the Diemerdijk. Ca. 1650–53. Pen and wash in bistre, white body color, on greyish paper. 76 x 244 mm. Chatsworth Settlement.

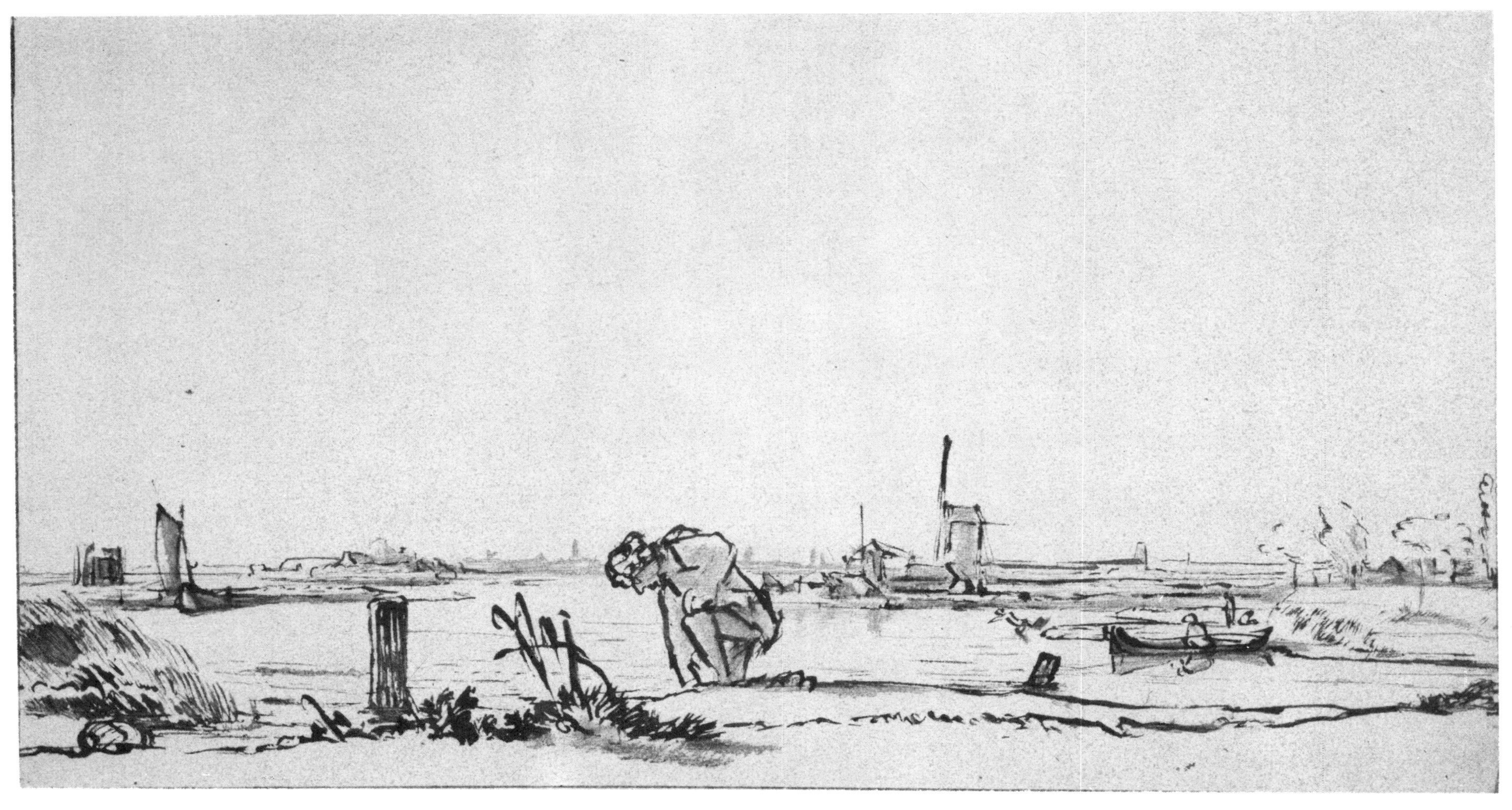

41. A View of the Amstel with a Man Bathing; in the Background Amsterdam. Ca. 1650–55. Reed pen and wash in bistre, white body color. 146 x 273 mm. Kupferstichkabinett, Berlin.

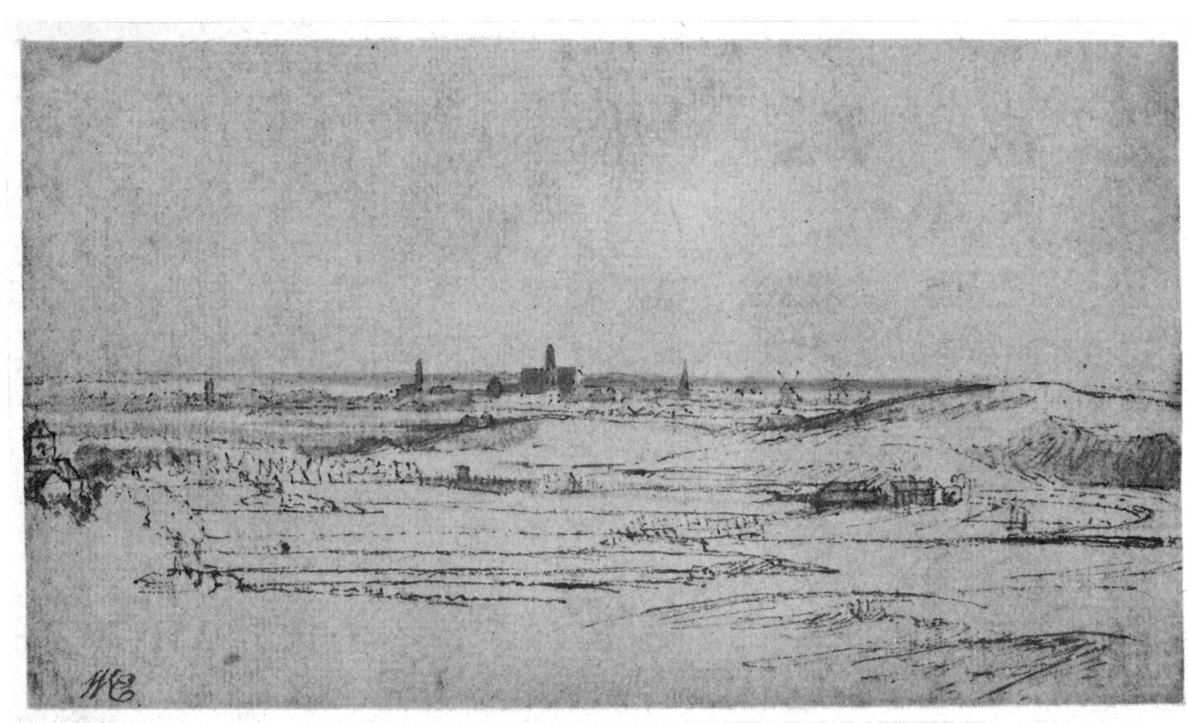

42. View of Haarlem Seen from Overveen. Ca. 1651. Pen and bistre, wash. 89 x 152 mm. Boymans-van Beuningen Museum, Rotterdam.

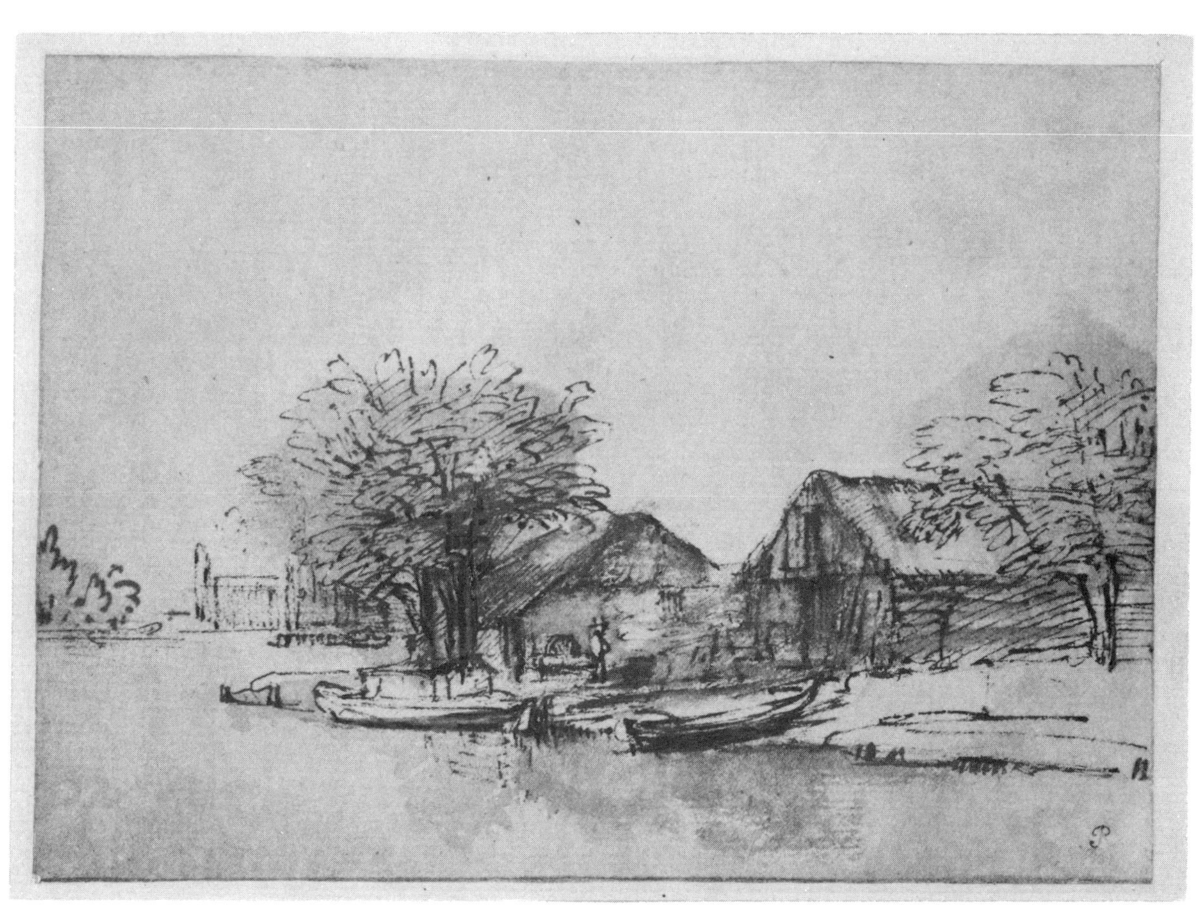

43. COTTAGES BY THE WATER. Ca. 1652. Pen and bistre. 110 x 149 mm. Museum, Groningen.

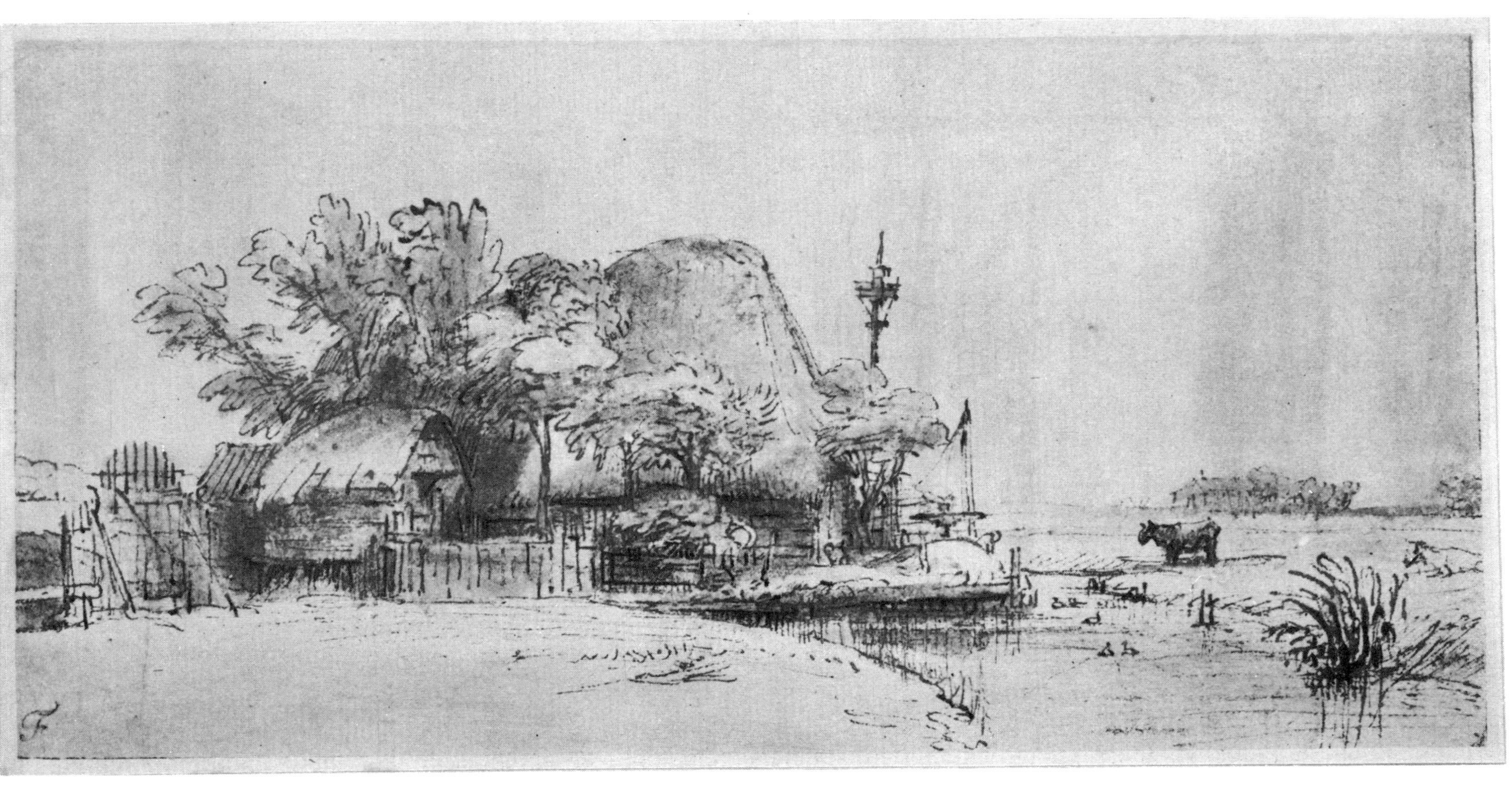

44. A Farmstead Beside a Stream. Ca. 1652. Reed pen and bistre, wash. 108 x 220 mm. Chatsworth Settlement.

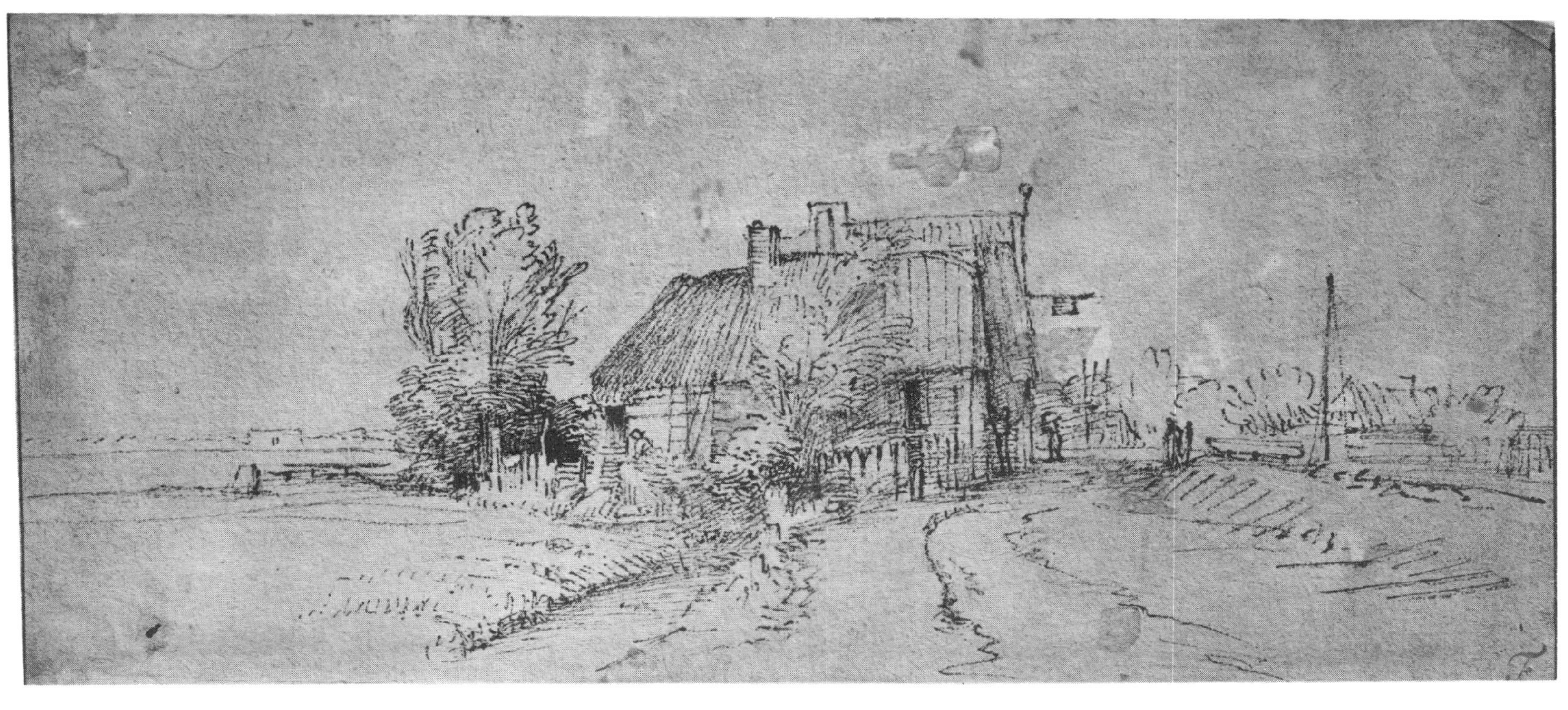

45. An Inn Beside a Road. Ca. 1652. Pen and bistre, on light grey prepared paper. 100 x 226 mm. Chatsworth Settlement.

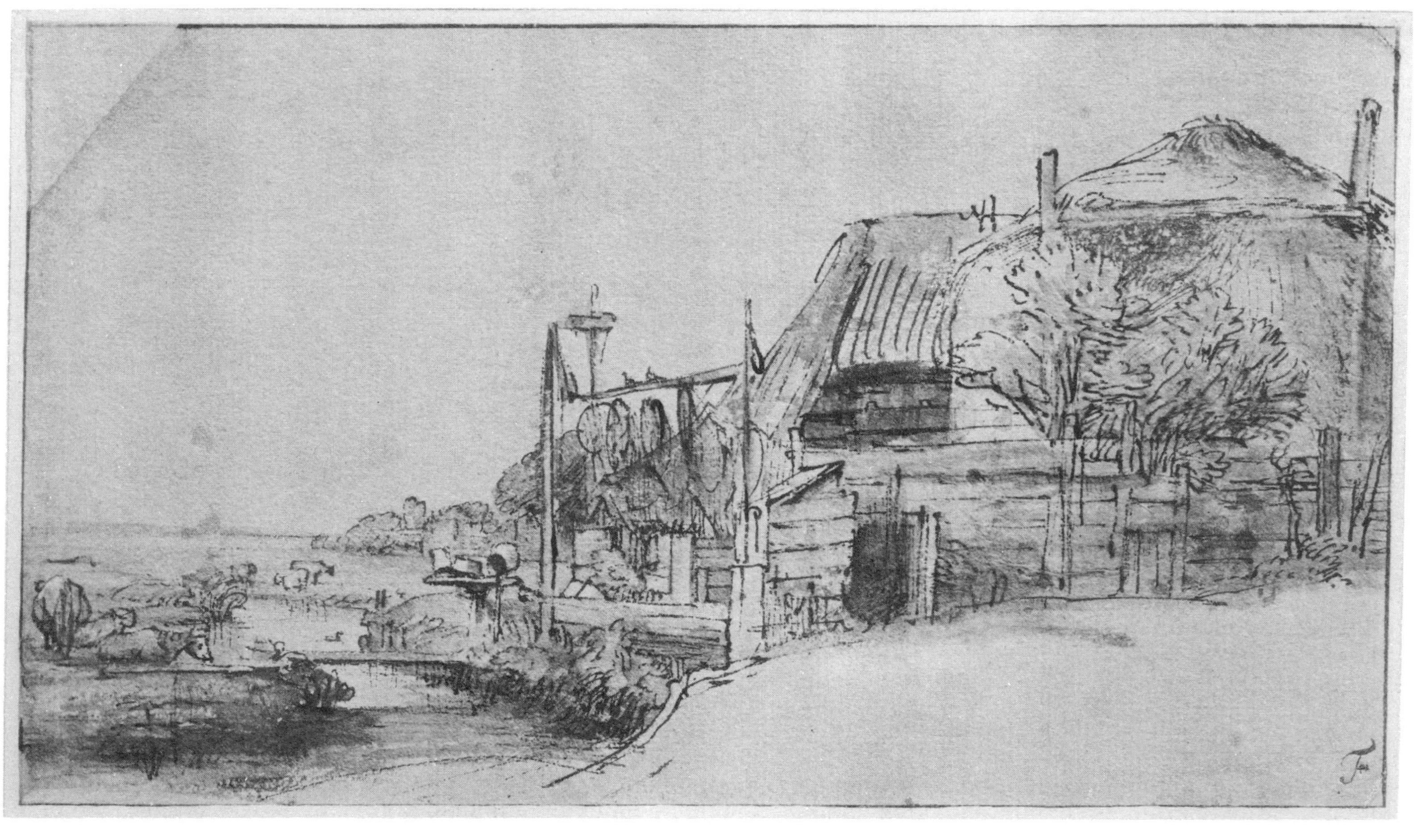

46. A Farmstead with a Hayrick and Weirs Beside a Stream. Ca. 1652. Reed pen and bistre, wash, white body color. 116 x 202 mm. Chatsworth Settlement.

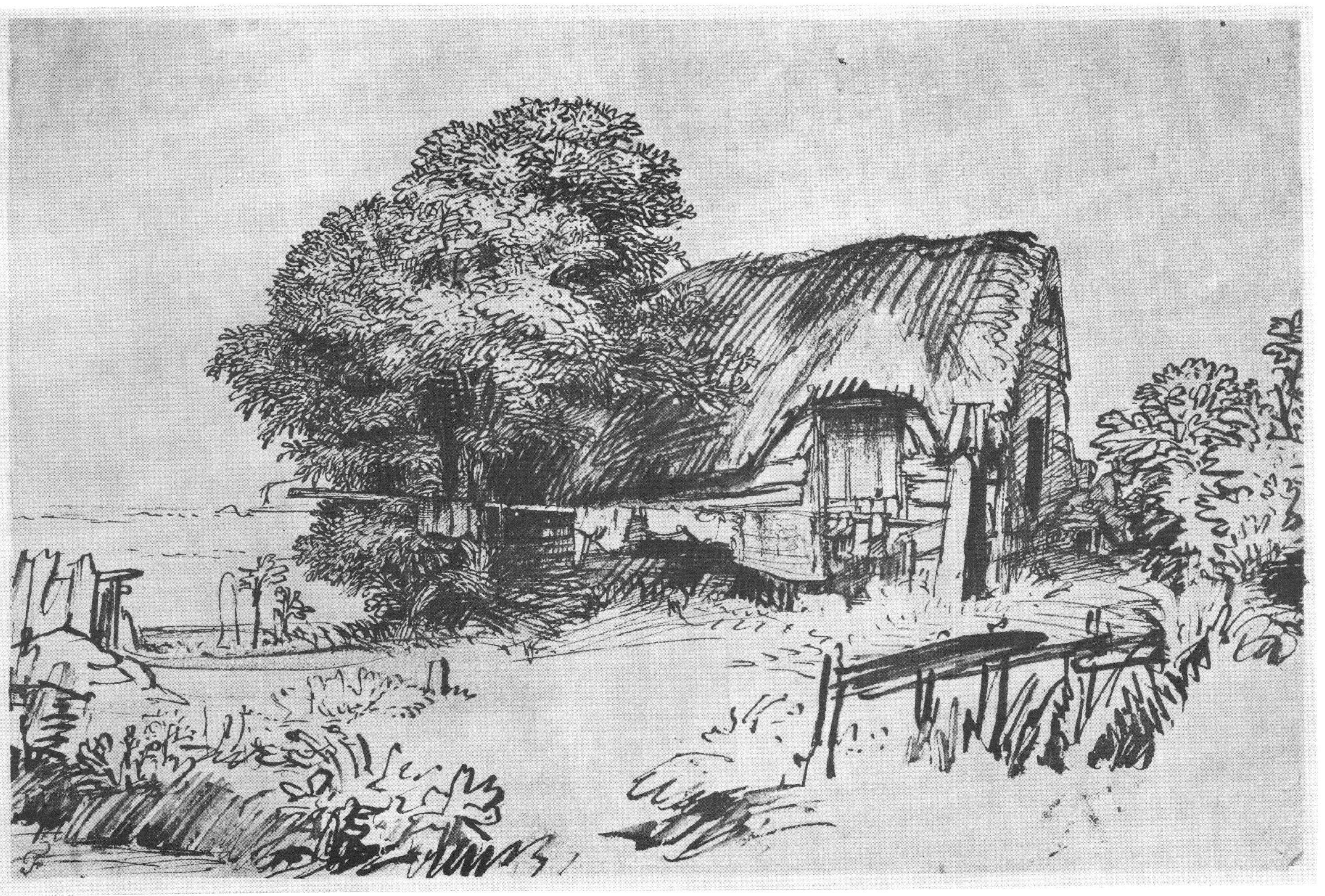

47 A Thatched Cottage by a Tree. Ca. 1652. Reed pen and bistre. 175 x 267 mm. Chatsworth Settlement.

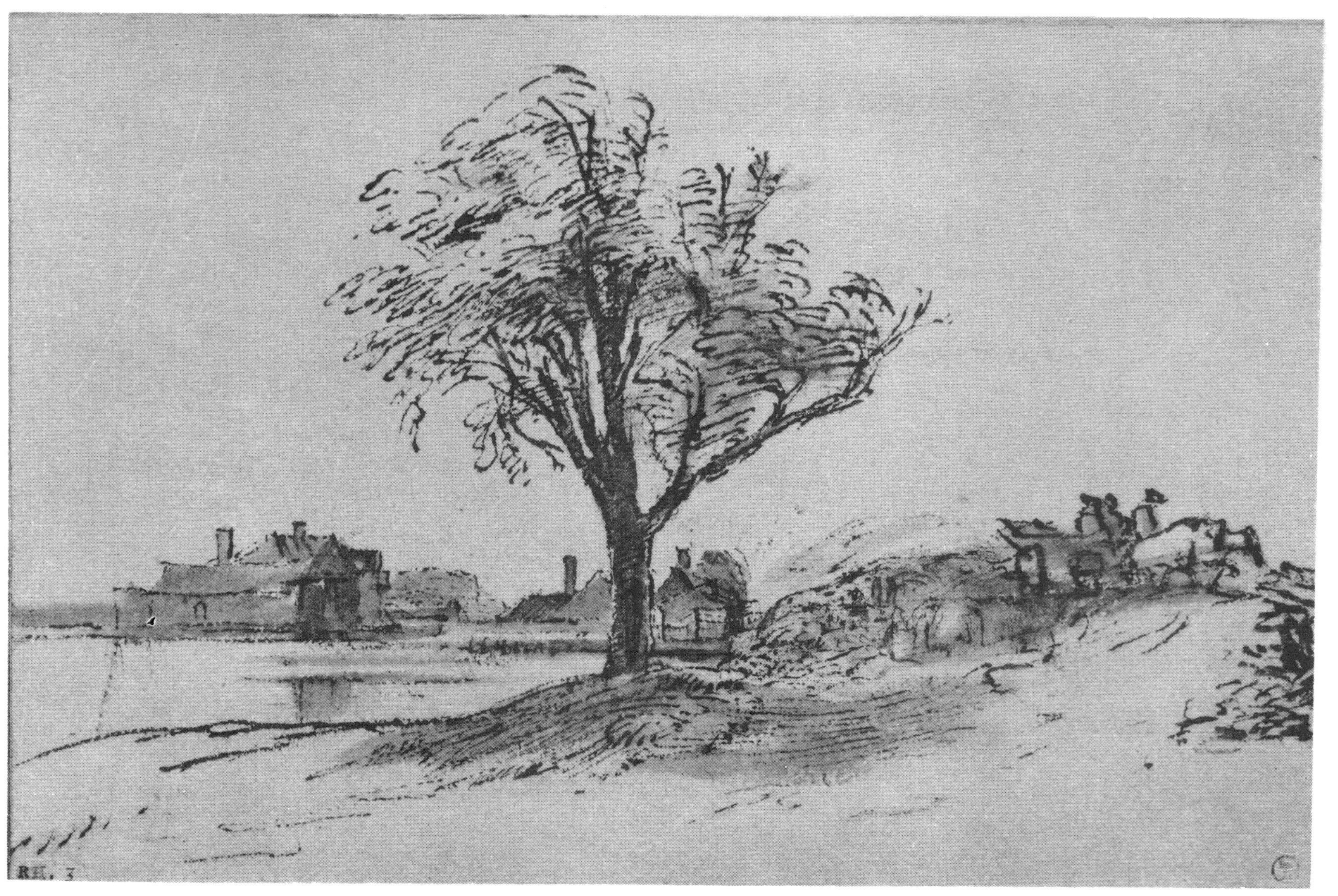

48. Large Tree on a Dike. Ca. 1652–55. Reed pen and wash in bistre. 150 x 231 mm. Louvre, Paris.

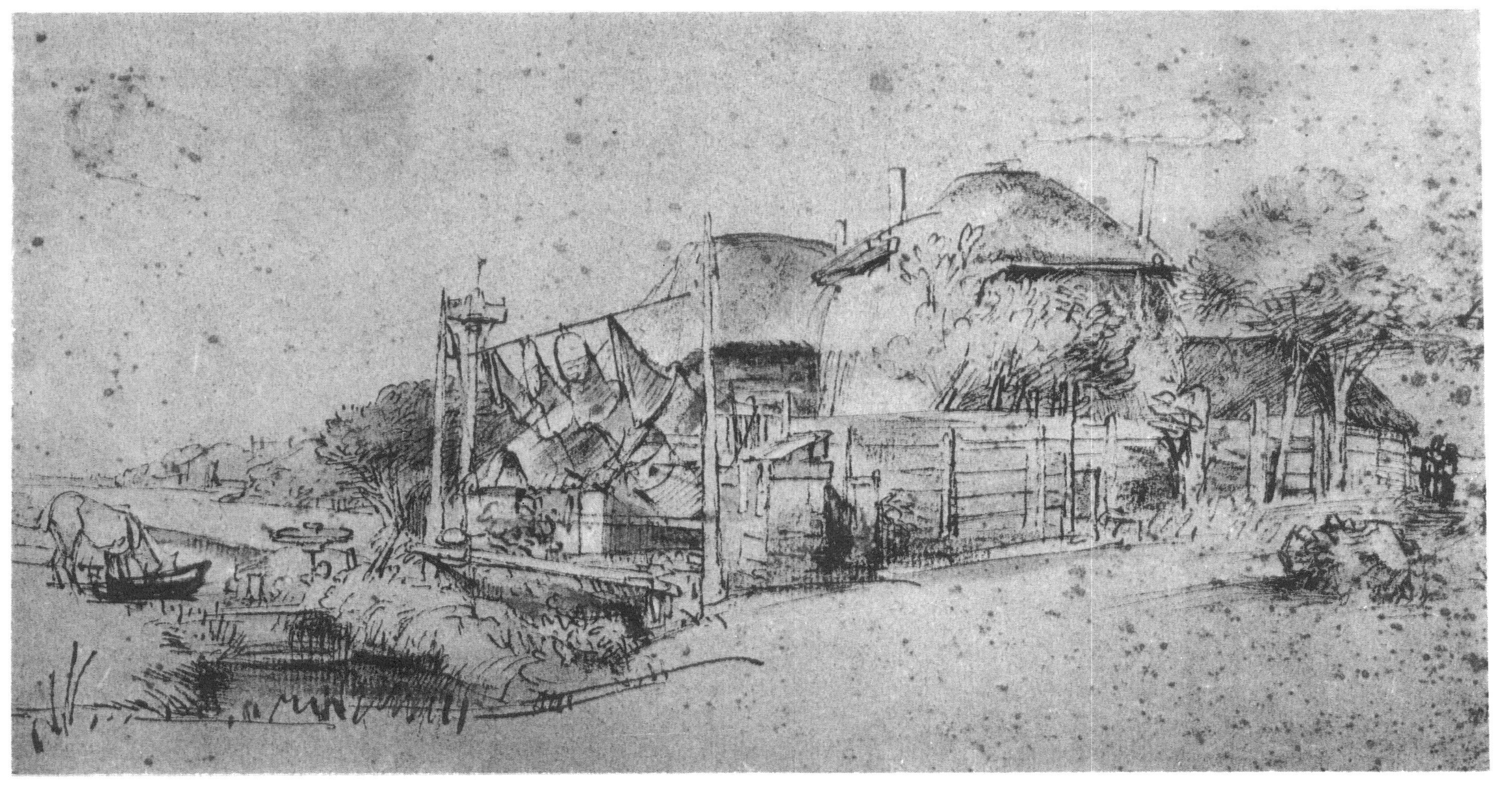

49. Farmstead with a Hayrick and Weirs. Ca. 1652. Pen and wash in bistre. 120 x 226 mm. Frits Lugt Collection, Paris.

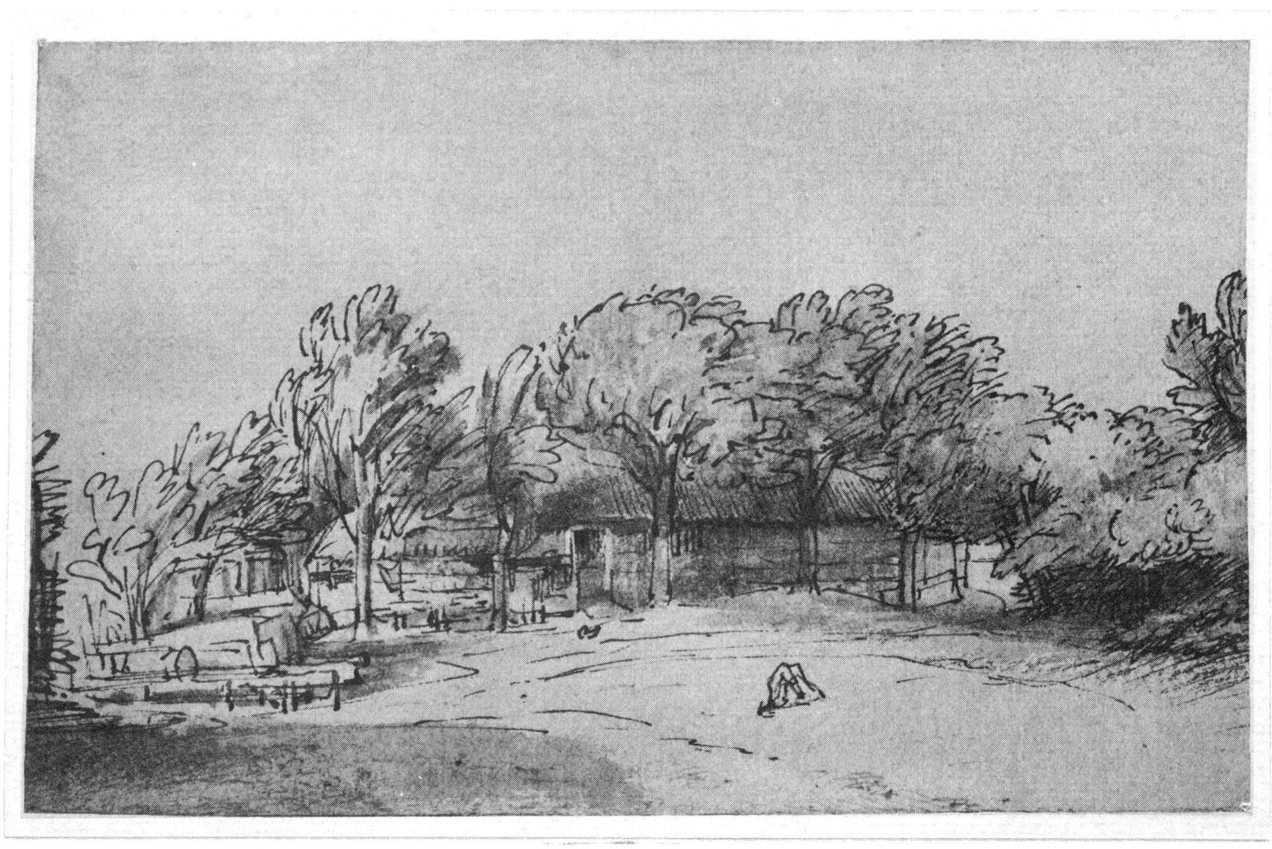

50. A Cottage and a Barn Surrounded by Trees. Ca. 1652. Pen and bistre, wash. 102 x 161 mm. Boymans-van Beuningen Museum, Rotterdam.

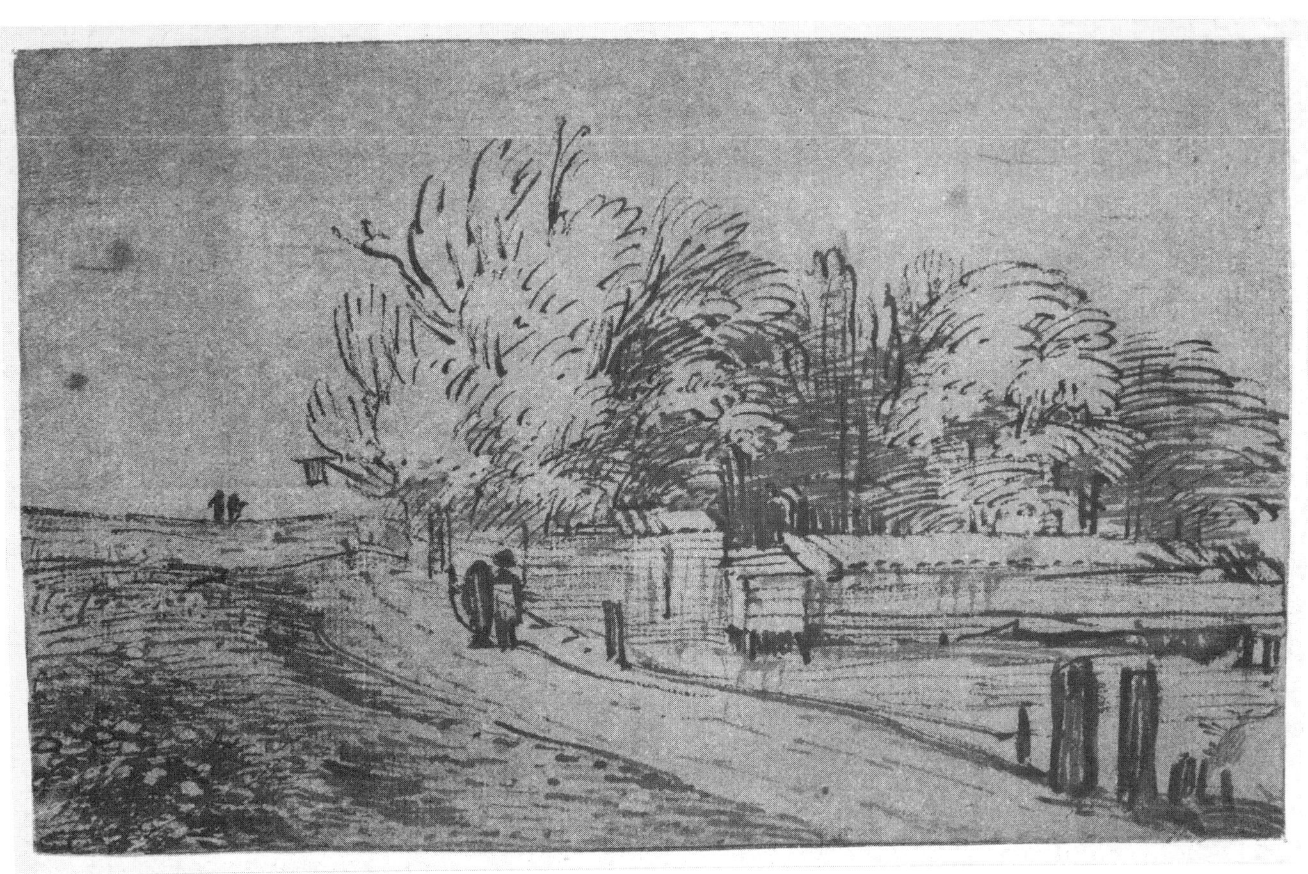

51. Landscape with a Road. Ca. 1653. Reed pen and bistre wash. 111 x 172 mm. British Museum, London.

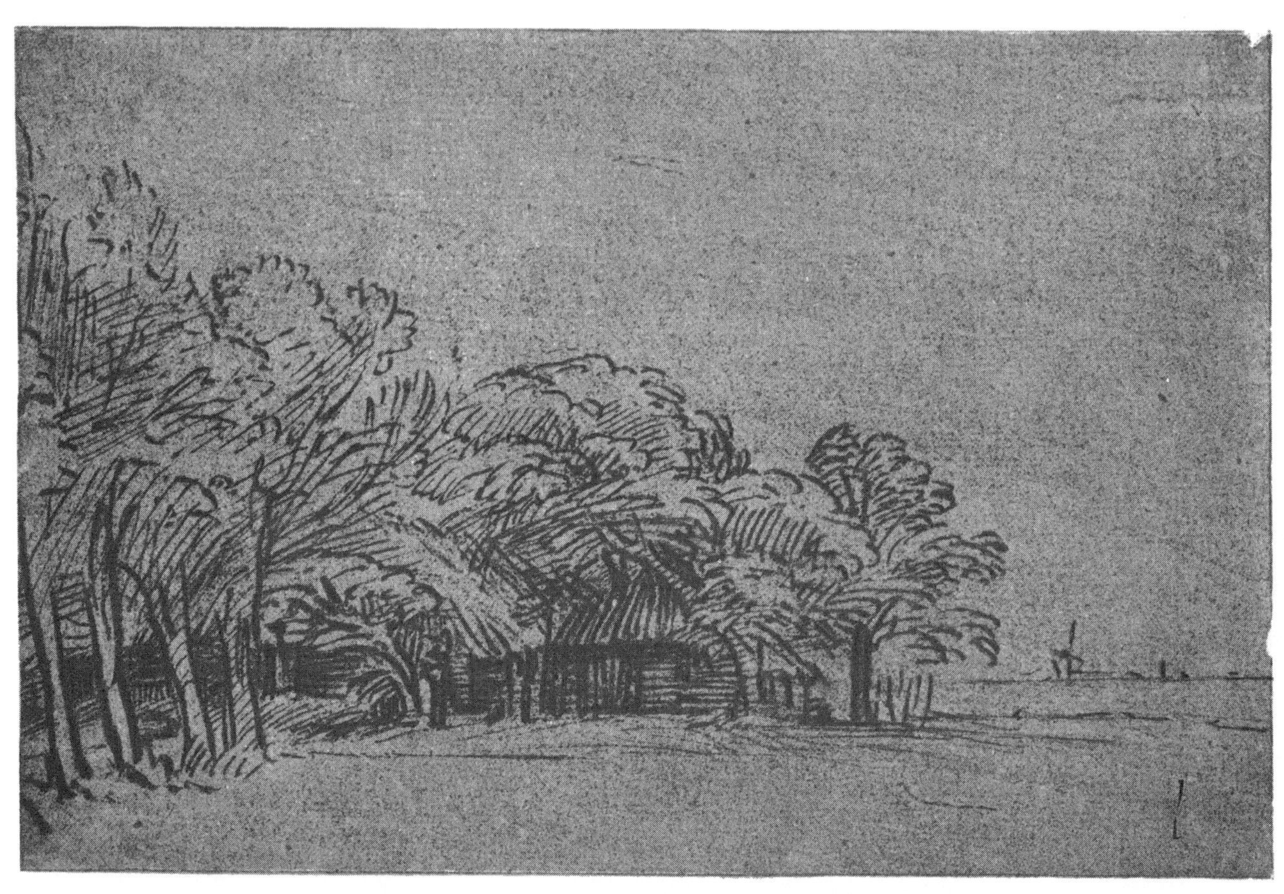

52. Cottages Among a Clump of Large Trees. Ca. 1653. Reed pen and bistre. 113 x 165 mm. Formerly J. P. Heseltine Collection, London.

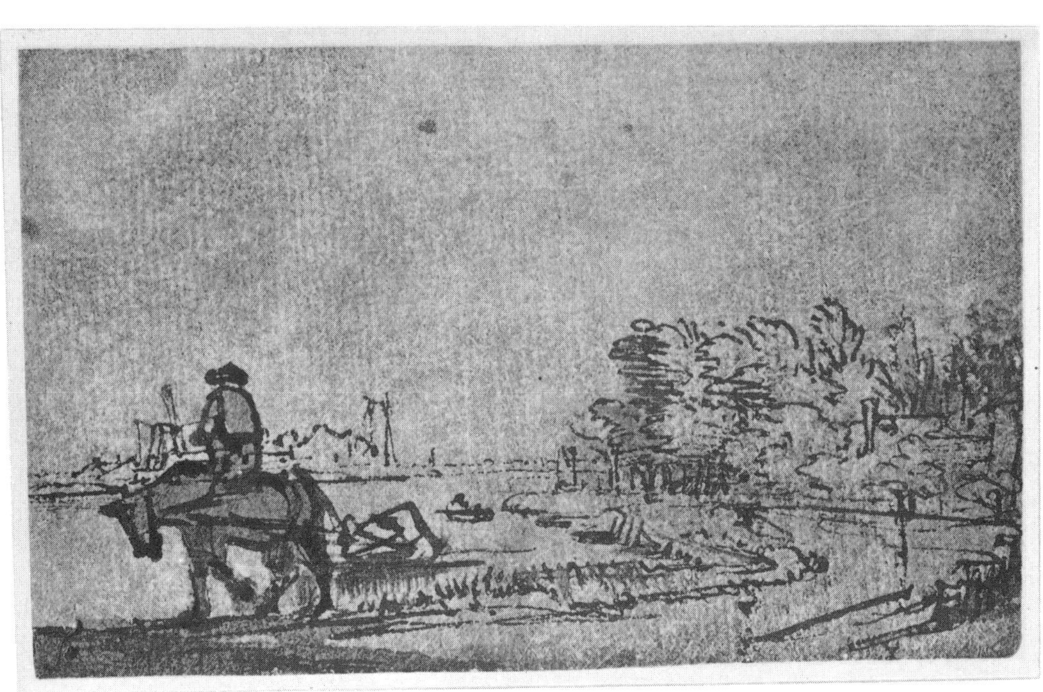

53. View Over the Amstel Near the Omval, with a Horse Towing a Boat. Ca. 1655. Pen and bistre, wash. 82 x 132 mm. Chatsworth Settlement.

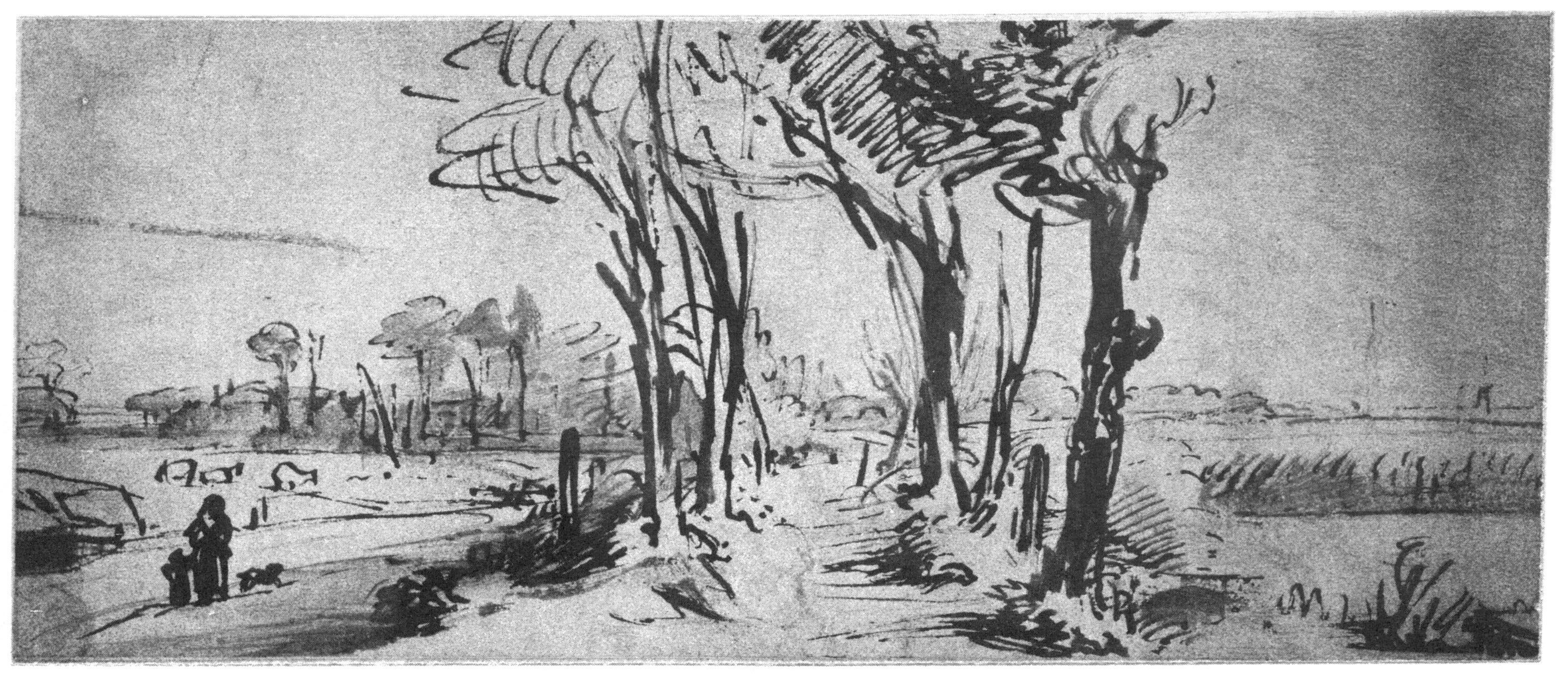

54. An Avenue of Trees Leading into the Distance. Ca. 1655. Reed pen and wash in bistre. 99 x 235 mm. Kupferstichkabinett, Berlin.

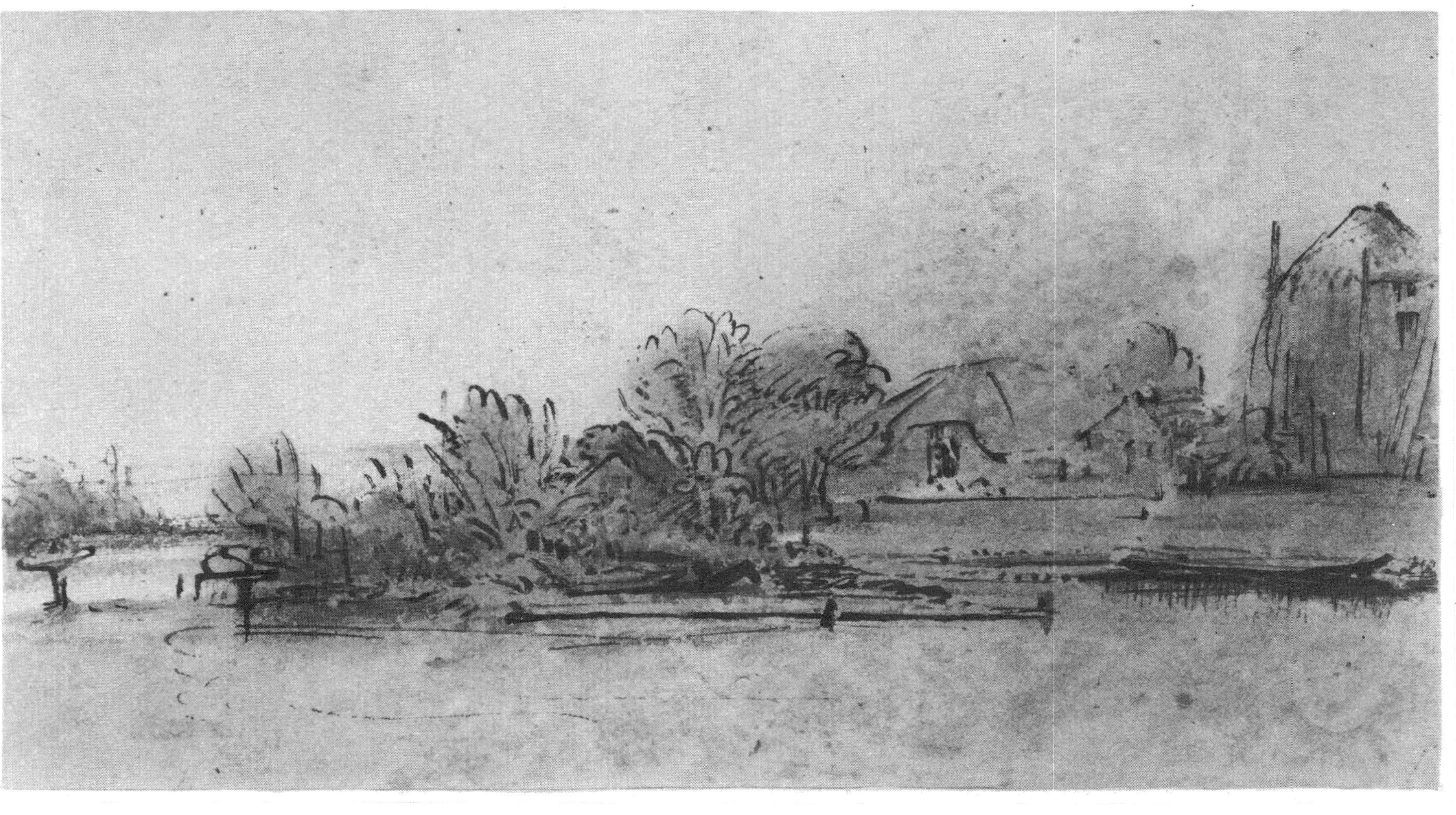

55. Riverside Landscape, a Cottage and High Hayrick to the Right. Ca. 1655. Reed pen and bistre, wash. 132 x 239 mm. British Museum, London.

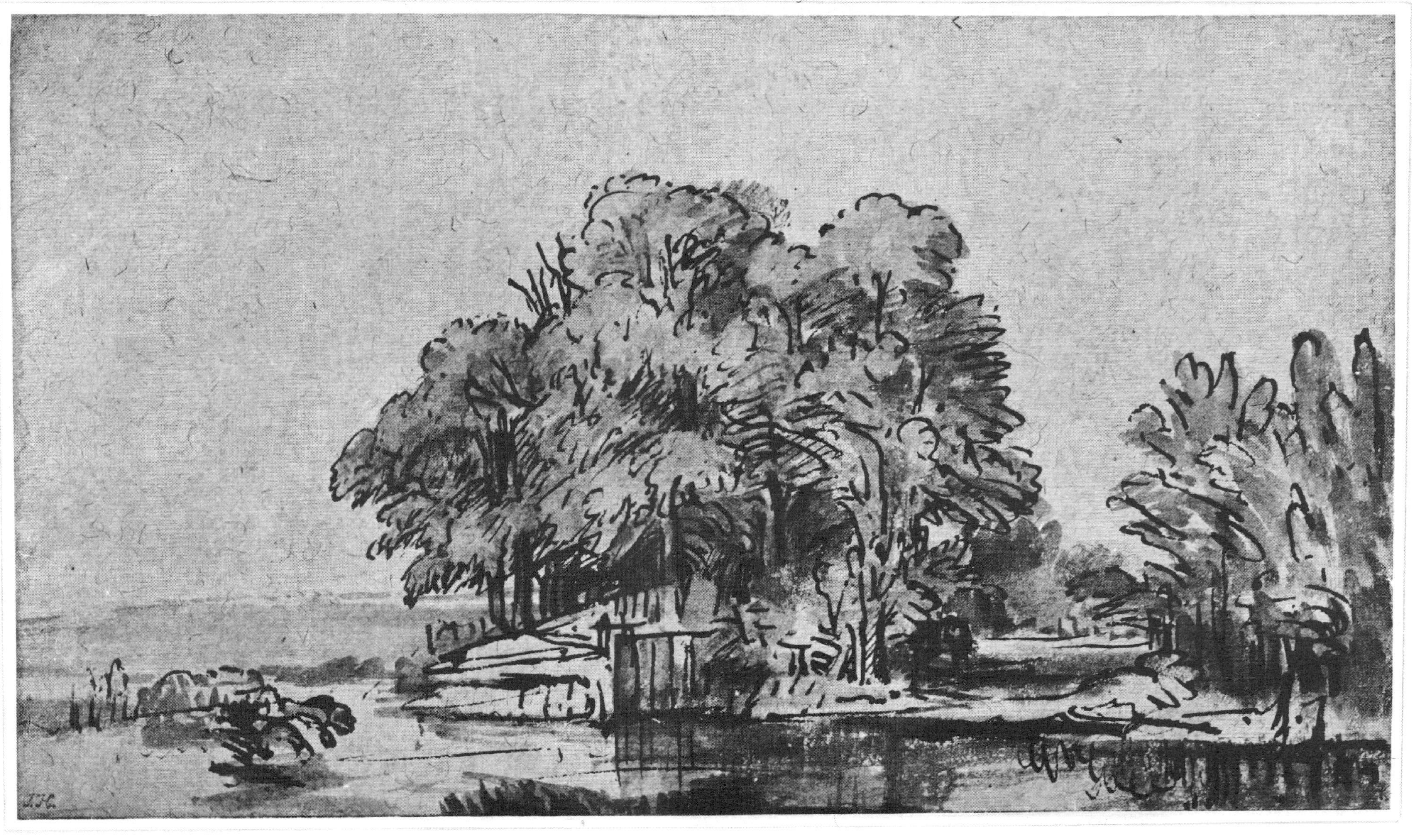

56. A Group of Large Trees on the Edge of a Pond. Ca. 1655. Pen and bistre, wash. 145 x 250 mm. Louvre, Paris.

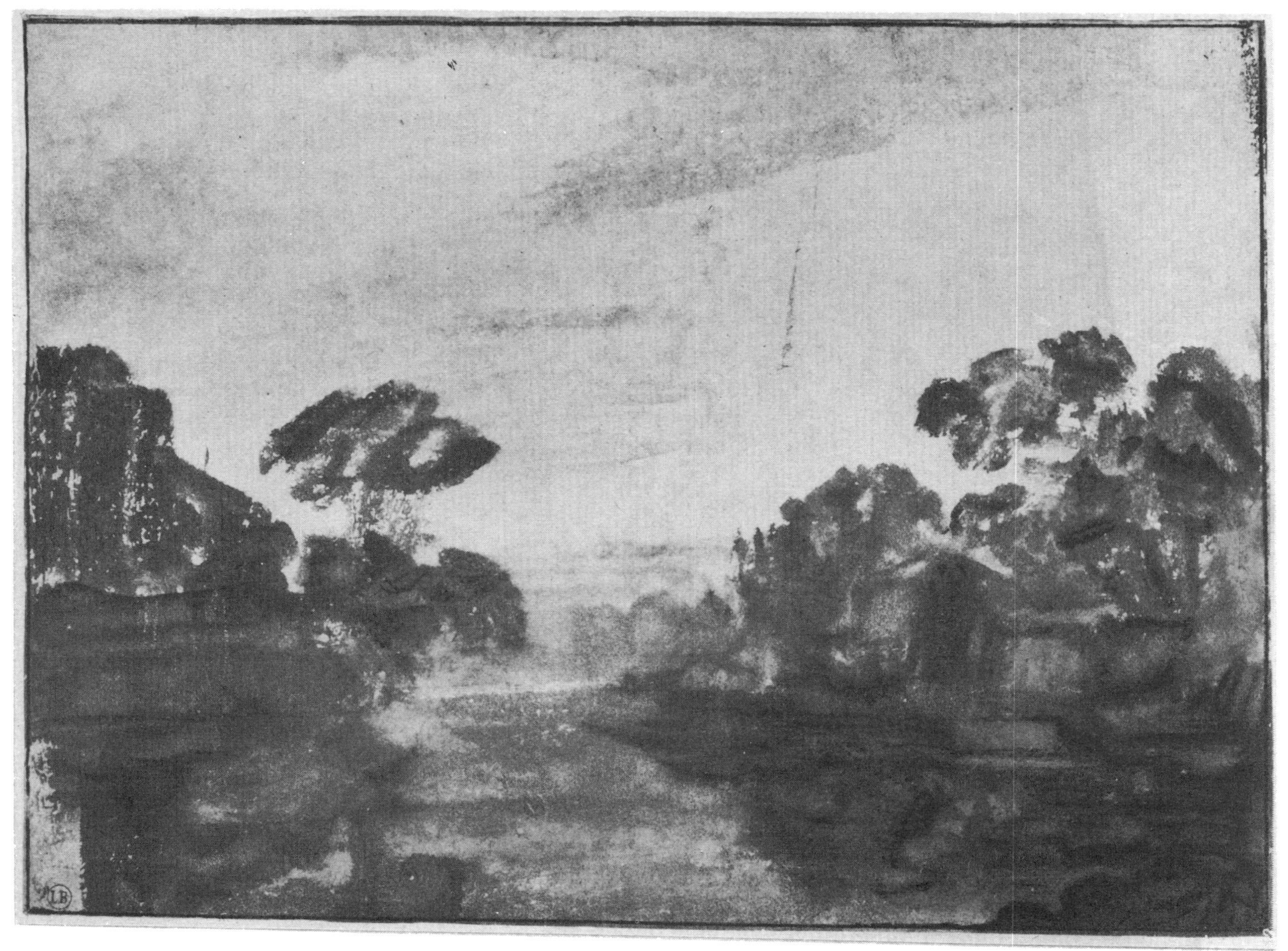

57. RIVER WITH TREES ON ITS EMBANKMENT AT DUSK. Ca. 1655. Brush and bistre. 136 x 187 mm. Louvre, Paris.

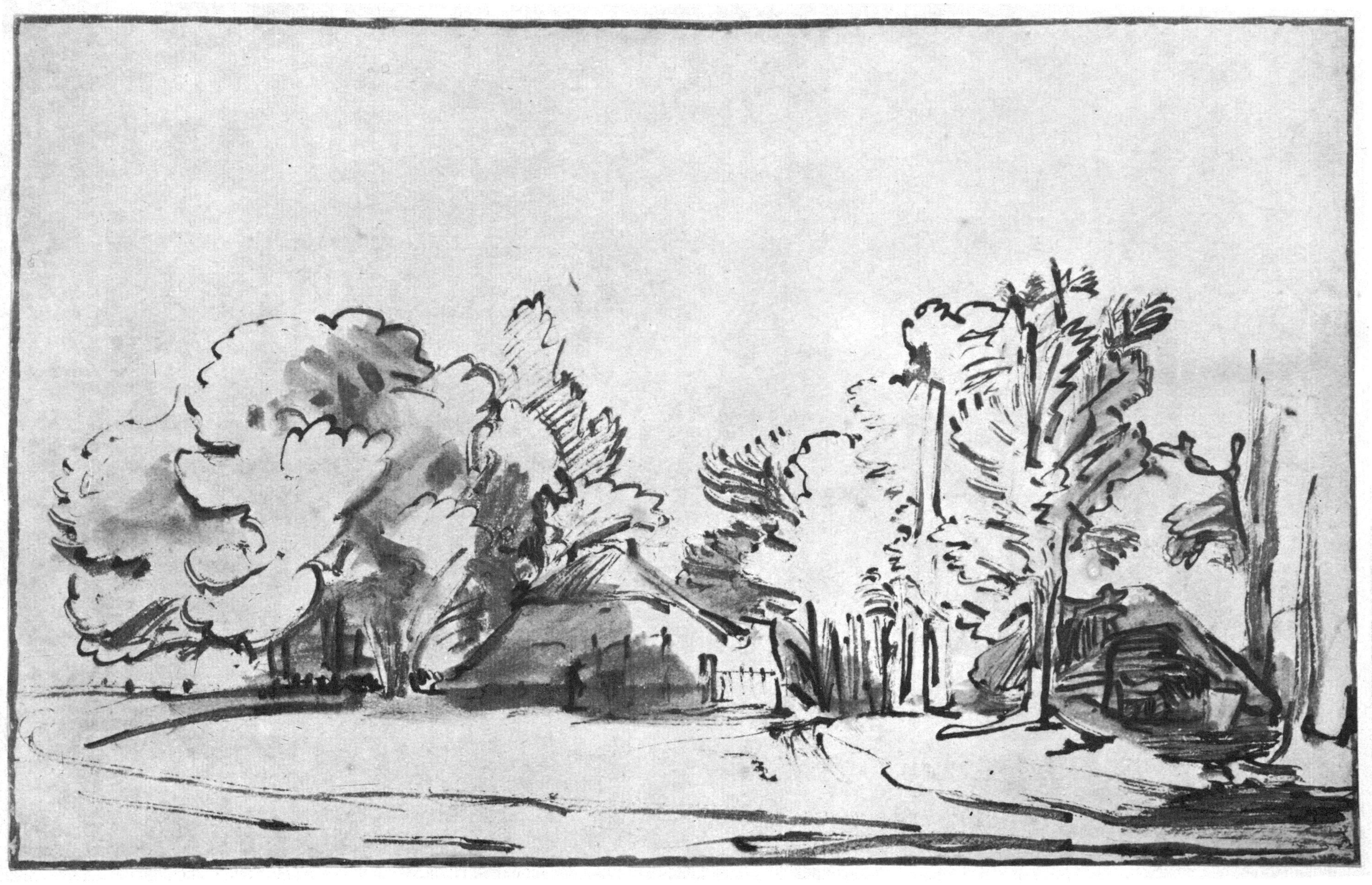

58. Cottages Amongst High Trees. Ca. 1655–60. Pen and brush in bistre, wash. 195 x 310 mm. Kupferstichkabinett, Berlin.

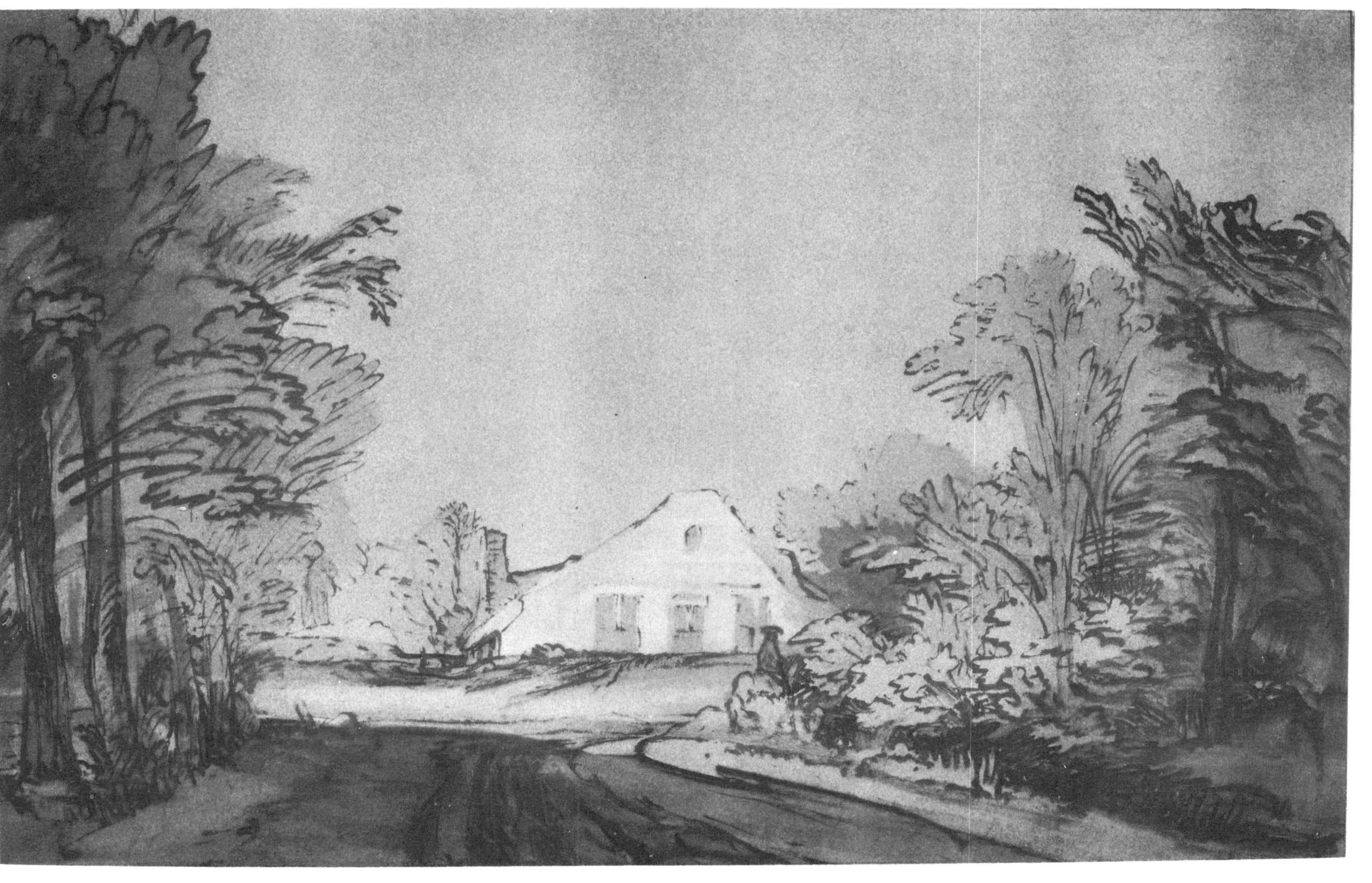

59. House Beside a Road Lined with Trees. Ca. 1657–60. Reed pen and wash in bistre. 210 x 330 mm. Frits Lugt Collection, Paris.